# THE CHIGNECTO ISTHMUS
# AND ITS FIRST SETTLERS

# THE CHIGNECTO ISTHMUS AND ITS FIRST SETTLERS

## HOWARD TRUEMAN

ISBN: 978-93-5614-119-3

Published:        1902

**LECTOR HOUSE LLP**
E-MAIL: lectorpublishing@gmail.com

Fort Cumberland in 1850

# THE CHIGNECTO ISTHMUS AND ITS FIRST SETTLERS

BY

## HOWARD TRUEMAN

1902

# PREFACE

For some years past I, in common with many others, have felt that all letters of interest and accessible facts in connection with the early history of the Truemans should be collected and put in permanent form, not because there is anything of interest to the general public in the records of a family whose members have excelled, if at all, in private rather than in public life, but in order that the little knowledge there is of the early history of the family might not pass forever out of the reach of later generations with the death of those whose memory carries them back to the original settlers. In getting together material necessary for the work, numbers of interesting facts concerning other families came inevitably to light. In order to preserve these facts, and at the same time give the book a slightly wider interest, I decided to write a short history of those families connected by marriage with the first and second generations of Truemans, and also, as far as material was available, of the first settlers in the old township of Cumberland, which now includes the settlements of Fort Lawrence, Westmoreland Point, Point de Bute, Jolicure, Bay Road, Bay Verte, Upper Tidnish and Port Elgin. Finally, as a kind of setting for the whole, I have prefaced these records with a brief outline of the early history of the Isthmus.

That the work falls far below the ideal goes without saying. Anyone who has made the effort to collect facts of local history knows how difficult it is to get reliable information. In almost every case where there was a conflict of opinion I have endeavored to verify my facts by light thrown on them from different directions; but doubtless mistakes will be found. By keeping the work in preparation for a longer time, more matter of interest could certainly be added, and perhaps corrections made; but to this there is no end, as the discovery of every new item of interest reveals a whole series more to investigate.

To all who have given me assistance warmest thanks are tendered. To Dr. Ganong, of Northampton, Mass.; Judge Morse, Amherst; W. C. Milner, Sackville; and Dr. Steel of Amherst, grateful acknowledgment is especially due for their ready and cheerful help. To Murdoch's Nova Scotia, Hannay's Acadia and to Dixon's and Black's family histories I have also been indebted.

# CONTENTS

# LIST OF ILLUSTRATIONS

*Page*

# INTRODUCTION

THIS book needs no introduction to the people of the Isthmus, whom it will most interest. I shall therefore attempt only to point out the plan the present work will take in the general history of Eastern Canada.

Mr. Trueman does not profess to have attempted a complete history of the Isthmus. The earlier periods, prior to the coming of the Yorkshiremen, are so replete with interest that a many times larger work than the present would be necessary for their full consideration, but Mr. Trueman has treated them with sufficient fulness to show the historical conditions of the country into which the Yorkshiremen came. It is the history of these Yorkshiremen and their descendants which Mr. Trueman treats so fully and authoritatively, and withal, from a local standpoint, so interestingly; and his work is the more valuable for the reason that hitherto but little has been published upon this subject. Some articles have appeared in local newspapers, and there are references to it in the provincial histories, but no attempt has hitherto been made to treat the subject as it deserves. Those of us who are interested in history from a more scientific standpoint will regret that the material, particularly of the earlier part of the Yorkshire immigration could not have been more documentary and less traditional, but that it is as here given is not Mr. Trueman's fault but a result of the nature of the case. It is not impossible, by the way, that such documents may yet be discovered, perhaps in some still unsuspected archives. It is to be remembered, however, that to a local audience, documents are of less interest than tradition, and the genealogical phases of history, here so fully treated, are most interesting of all. Mr. Trueman seems to have sifted the traditions with care, and he certainly has devoted to his task an unsurpassed knowledge of his subject, much loving labor, and no small enthusiasm. I believe the local readers of his work will agree with me that this history could not have fallen into more appropriate hands.

It does not seem to me that Mr. Trueman has exaggerated the part played by the Yorkshiremen and their descendants in our local history. While it is doubtless too much to say that their loyalty saved Nova Scotia (then including New Brunswick) to Great Britain by their steadfastness at the time of the Eddy incident in 1776, there can be no doubt that it contributed largely to that result and rendered easy the suppression of an uprising which would have given the authorities very great trouble had it succeeded. But there can be no question whatever as to the value to the Chignecto region, and hence to all this part of Canada, of this immigration of God-fearing, loyal, industrious, progressive Yorkshiremen. Although they and their descendants have not occupied the places in life of greatest prominence, they have been none the less useful citizens in contributing as they have to the solid foundations of the upbuilding of a great people.

It is of interest in this connection to note that Mr. Trueman's book, although preceded in Nova Scotia by several county histories, is for New Brunswick, with one or two exceptions (in Jack's "History of the City of St. John," and Lorimer's pamphlet, "History of the Passamaquiddy Islands") the first history of a limited portion of the Province to appear in book form, although valuable newspaper series on local history have been published. May it prove the leader of a long series of such local histories which, let us hope, will not cease to appear until every portion of these interesting Provinces has been adequately treated.

W. F. GANONG.

# CHAPTER I
## THE CHIGNECTO ISTHMUS

THE discovery of America added nearly a third to the then known land surface of the earth, and opened up two of its richest continents. If such an extent of territory were thrown into the world's market to-day, the rapidity with which it would be exploited and explored, and its wealth made tributary to the world's requirements, would astonish, if they were here, the men who pioneered the settlement of the new country and left so royal a heritage to their descendants. To those who cross the Atlantic in the great ocean liners of our time, and think them none too safe, the fleet with which Sir Humphrey Gilbert crossed the sea to plant his colony in the new land must seem a frail protection indeed against the dangers of the western ocean.

Perhaps in no way can the progress made since the beginning of the nineteenth century be more forcibly brought before the mind than by comparing the immense iron steamships of the present day with the small wooden vessels with which commerce was carried on and battles were fought and won a hundred and fifty years ago.

The Isthmus of Chignecto separates the waters of the Bay of Fundy from those of Bay Verte, and constitutes the neck of land which saves Nova Scotia from being an island. It is seventeen miles between the two bays at the narrowest point, and considering the town of Amherst the south-eastern limit, and the village of Sackville the north-western, it may be put down as a little less than ten miles in width.

The southern slope is drained by four tidal rivers or creeks, namely, La Planche, Missiquash, Aulac and the Tantramar. These rivers empty into Cumberland Basin, and their general course is from north-east to south-west. In length they are from twelve to fifteen miles, and run through narrow valleys, the soil of which is made up largely from a rich sediment carried by the tide from the muddy waters of the basin. These valleys are separated from each other by ridges of high land ranging from one hundred to one hundred and fifty feet above the sea level.

The Tidnish River, and several streams emptying into the Bay Verte, drain the Isthmus on its northern slope. The Missiquash and Tidnish rivers, each for some part of its course, form the boundary between the provinces of Nova Scotia and New Brunswick. The tides at the head of the Bay of Fundy rise to the height of sixty feet, or even higher, and are said to be the highest in the world. The mud deposit from the overflow of these tidal waters, laid down along the river valleys, is from one foot to eighty feet deep, varying as the soil beneath rises and falls.

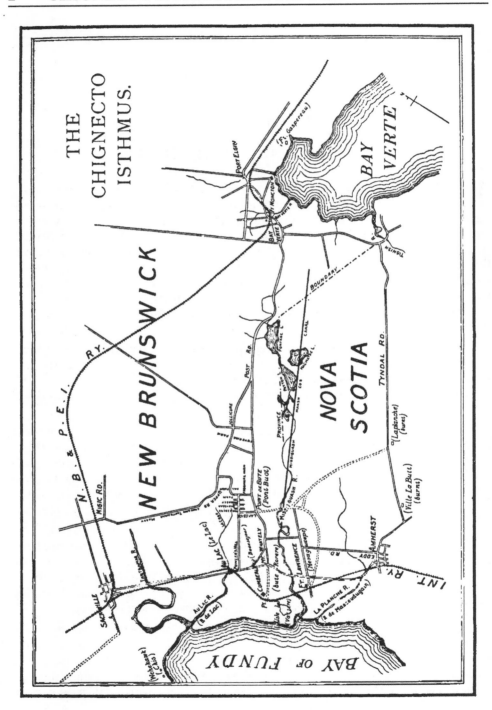

Map of Chignecto Isthmus

Between Sackville and Amherst there is an area of some fifty thousand acres of these alluvial lands, reclaimed and unreclaimed. Some of this marsh has been cutting large crops of hay for one hundred and fifty years, and there is no evidence of diminished fertility, although no fertilizer has been used in that time; other sections have become exhausted and the tide has been allowed to overflow them. This treatment will restore them to their original fertility.

Cartier was the first of the early navigators to drop anchor in a New Brunswick harbor. This was in the summer of 1534, and the place was on the Gulf of St. Lawrence, near the mouth of the Miramich River. This was on the 30th of June. Landing the next day and finding the country well wooded, he was delighted and spoke of it in glowing terms.

The first white men to visit the Isthmus with a view to trade and settlement came from Port Royal in the summer of 1612.

In 1670, Jacob Bourgeois, a resident of Port Royal, and a few other restless spirits, were the first to make a permanent settlement. These were followed by another contingent under the leadership of Pierre Arsenault.

In 1676, the King of France gave a large grant of territory in Acadia to a French nobleman, Michael Le Neuf, Sieur de La Valliere. This grant included all the Chignecto Isthmus. Tonge's Island, a small islet in the marsh near the mouth of the Missiquash River, is called Isle La Valliere on the old maps, and was probably occupied by La Valliere himself when he lived on the Isthmus.

From this date Chignecto began to take a prominent place in the history of Acadia, and continued for a hundred and fifty years to be one of the principal centres of influence under the rule both of France and Great Britain.

It was here that France made her last stand for the possession of Acadia. It was here that Jonathan Eddy, twenty years later, raised the standard of the revolted colonies, and made a gallant but unsuccessful effort to carry Nova Scotia over to the rebel cause.

From 1713 to 1750 was the most prosperous period of the French occupation. The population increased rapidly for those times. The market at Louisbourg furnished an outlet for the surplus produce of the soil. The wants of the people were few. The Acadians were thrifty and frugal, the rod and gun supplying a large part of the necessaries of life in many a home. The complaint was made by those who at that time were interested in the circulation of the King's silver that the people hoarded it up, and once they got possession of it the public were never allowed to see it again. The houses were small and destitute of many of the furnishings their descendants now think indispensable, but perhaps they enjoyed life quite as well as those of later generations.

Bay Verte at this time was a place of considerable importance. The Abbe Le Loutre lived here a part of the time, and owned a store kept by an agent. The trade between Quebec and Louisbourg and the settlements on the Isthmus was carried on through the Port of Bay Verte, and from there the farmers of Chignecto shipped their cattle and farm products. The Acadians were quick to see the benefits that would arise from reclaiming the rich river valleys, and they drew their revenues chiefly from this land. They did not readily take to the cutting down of the forests and preparing the upland for growing crops; they were more at home with the dyking-spade than the axe. A description of their methods of dyking and constructing aboideaux, written in 1710, is interesting to those who are doing the same work now.

The writer of 1710 says: "They stopped the current of the sea by creating large dykes, which they called aboideaux. The method was to plant five or six large trees in the places where the sea enters the marshes, and between each row to lay down other trees lengthways on top of each other, and fill the vacant places with mud so well beaten down that the tide could not pass through it. In the middle they adjusted a flood-gate in such a way as to allow the water from the marsh to flow out at low water without permitting the water from the sea to flow in at high tide." The writer adds that the work was expensive, but the second year's crop repaid them for the outlay. This is more than can be said for present-day experience in the same kind of work.

The land reclaimed on the Aulac was confined principally to the upper portion of the river. The Abbe Le Loutre saw that the benefit would be great if this river were dammed near its mouth, and he was at work at a large aboideau, for which he had received money from France, when the fall of Beausejour forever put a stop to his enterprise.

Wheat seems to have grown very abundantly on the marsh when it was first dyked, judging from the census reports of those days and the traditions handed down.

The old French maps of 1750 and earlier show settlements at Beaubassin (Fort Lawrence), Pont a Buot (Point de Bute), Le Lac (Jolicure), We-He-Kauk (Westcock), We-He-Kauk-Chis (Little Westcock), Tantramar (Upper Sackville), Pre Du Bourge (Middle Sackville), We-He-Kage (Amherst Point) and Amherst or Upper Amherst, Vill-La-Butte, and La Planche. There were settlements also at Maccan, Nappan and Minudie. The statement that the village of Beaubassin, in 1750, contained a hundred and forty houses, and a population numbering a thousand, seems improbable under the circumstances.

Fort Lawrence, the site of old Beaubassin, contains to-day less than forty houses, and not more than three hundred inhabitants, yet more land is under cultivation now than in any previous time in its history. It is highly probable that the whole population on the south side of the Isthmus was reckoned as belonging to Beaubassin.

There is good reason for saying that the population of the district embraced in the parish of Westmoreland, excepting Port Elgin, was much larger from 1750 to 1755 than it has ever been since.

The Seigneur La Valliere was, no doubt, the most prominent man, politically, on the Isthmus during the French period. He was appointed commandant of Acadia in 1678, by Count Frontenac, and just missed being made governor. He was a man of broader views than most of his contemporaries. He encouraged trade, and was willing that others beside his own countrymen should reap the benefits if they were ready to pay the price. He anticipated the *modus vivendi* system now in force between this country and the United States in dealing with the fisheries, and instead of keeping a large fleet to patrol the coast and drive the English from the fishing ground, he charged them a license fee of five pistoles (about twenty-five dollars) for each vessel, thus giving them a free hand in the business.

La Valliere's farm was probably on the island marked on the old maps, "Isle La Valliere," and here he lived when not in other parts of the colony on public business. He had a son called Beaubassin, who was always ready to take a hand in any expedition that required courage and promised danger. In 1703, this Beaubassin was the leader of a party of French and Indians that attacked Casco and would have captured the place but for the timely arrival of a British man-of-war.

On the 11th April, 1713, the Treaty of Utrecht was signed. This gave all Nova Scotia, or Acadia, comprehended within its ancient boundaries, as also the city of Port Royal, now called Annapolis Royal, to the Queen of Great Britain. The English claimed this to include all the territory east of a line drawn from north of the Kennebec River to Quebec, taking in all the south shore of the St. Lawrence, Gaspe, the Island of St. John, and Cape Breton. The French contended that Acadia only included the southern half of the present Province of Nova Scotia. Views so divergent held by the contracting parties to an agreement, could scarcely fail to produce irritation and ultimately result in war.

In 1740, the Abbe Le Loutre, Vicar-General of Acadia under the Bishop of Quebec, and missionary to the Micmacs, came to Acadia to take charge of his mission. It soon became apparent that the Rev. Father was more anxious to advance the power and prestige of the King of France than he was to minister to the spiritual elevation of the benighted Indians. The course pursued by the Abbe defeated the end he had in view. His aim was to make Acadia a French colony; but in reality he helped to make it the most loyal British territory in North America.

The successful raid of de Villiers, in the winter of 1747, convinced the English that so long as Chignecto was in possession of the French, and was used as a base of operations to defy the English Government, there could be no lasting peace or security for settlers of British blood. Taking this view of the matter, Governor Cornwallis determined to take measures to drive the French from the Isthmus. The unsettled state of the French population through the Province contributed to this decision.

In November, 1754, Governor Lawrence wrote to Shirley, at Boston, that he had reason to believe the French were contemplating aggressive measures at Chignecto, and he thought it was quite time an effort was made to drive them from the north side of the Bay of Fundy. Col. Monckton carried this letter to Governor Shirley. The governor entirely agreed with the suggestion it contained, and had already taken some steps to bring about so desirable an end to the troubles the Government was experiencing on the Isthmus.

The matter was kept as secret as possible, but efforts were immediately made to raise a force to capture Fort Beausejour, the new fort built by the French on the high ground overlooking Beaubassin, on the north-west side of the Missiquash. So successful were they in getting up the expedition that, on the 23rd of May, everything was ready and the force set sail from Boston.

The expedition numbered two thousand men, under the command of Lieut.-Col. Monckton, with Lieutenants Winslow and Scott under him. They called at Annapolis, and were joined there by three hundred regulars of Warburton's regiment, and got a small train of artillery. Fort Lawrence[1] was reached on 2nd June, and the next day all the troops were landed and camped around the fort.

Vergor, the French General in command at Beausejour, called on all the Acadians capable of bearing arms to come into the fort and assist in its defence. The Acadians, however, would not obey this order unless Vergor would make a refusal to comply punishable with death. This would given them an excuse with which to meet the English if the fort were taken.

On the 4th June, the English broke camp and marched north from Fort Lawrence, a distance of about two miles along the ridge of high land; then, entering the Missiquash valley, they crossed over to Pont a Buot, or Buot's Bridge, which spanned the Missiquash River. This bridge was near what is now Point de Bute Corner. Here the French had a blockhouse garrisoned with thirty men. There was also a breastwork of timber. This place was defended for an hour by the French, and then, setting fire to the little fort, they left the English to cross over without opposition. The victorious force camped that night on the Point de Bute side of the Missiquash River.

At this day it is difficult to account for the slight value the Acadian seemed to place upon his home. He appears to have been always ready to set it on fire at the least danger of its falling into the hands of the English. The sixty houses that stood between Buot's Bridge and Beausejour all went up in flame that night, fired by the French soldiers as they retired before the English.

From the 4th until the 13th of June the English were engaged in cutting roads, building bridges, transporting cannon, and getting these into position north of the fort, on the high ground, within shelling distance. During this time the French had been strengthening their defences and making other arrangements for withstanding a seige (sic). The Abbe Le Loutre ceased work on his "abateau" and set his men to assist at the fort.

Scouting parties from either camp met once or twice, and the Indians captured an English officer named Hay, who was passing from Fort Lawrence to the English

[1] The fort at Fort Lawrence, was situate on the high land that separates the valleys of the Missiquash and La Planche rivers, a little less than two miles distant from Fort Beausejour. It was constructed in the month of September, 1750. Lieutenant-Colonel Lawrence arrived at the Isthmus with a strong force, consisting of the 48th Regiment, and three hundred men of the 45th Regiment. "The Indians and some of the French were rash enough to oppose the landing of so formidable a body of troops, but they were driven off after a sharp skirmish, in which the English lost about twenty killed and wounded." A short distance from where they landed Colonel Lawrence erected a picketal fort with block-houses, which was named for himself. A garrison of six hundred men was maintained here until the fall of Beausejour.

camp. On the 13th the English threw a few shells into the fort, and continued to shell the place on the 14th, without much apparent result. On that day Vergor received tidings that no help could be sent from Louisbourg. This news was more disastrous to the French than the English shells. The Acadians lost all heart and began to slip away into the woods and the settlements to the northward.

The next day, the 15th, larger shells were thrown, some falling into the fort. One shell killed the English officer, Hay, who was a prisoner, and several French officers, while they were at breakfast. This decided the matter. Vergor sent an officer to Monckton asking for a suspension of hostilities. That afternoon the following terms of surrender were agreed upon:

"1st. The commandant, officers, staff and others employed for the King and garrison of Beausejour, shall go out with arms and baggage, drums beating. 2nd. The garrison shall be sent to Louisbourg at the expense of the King of Great Britain. 3rd. The Governor shall have provisions sufficient to last them until they get to Louisbourg. 4th. As to the Acadians, as they were forced to bear arms under pain of death, they shall be pardoned. 5th. The garrison shall not bear arms in America for the space of six months. 6th. The foregoing are granted on condition that the garrison shall surrender to the troops of Great Britain by 7 p.m. this afternoon. Signed, Robert Monckton. At the camp before Beausejour, 16th June, 1755."

As soon as the British were in possession at Beausejour, Monckton sent a detachment of three hundred men, under Col. Winslow, to demand the surrender of the fort at Bay Verte. Capt. Villeray accepted the same terms as Vergor, and on the 18th of June, 1755, the Isthmus passed for ever out of the possession of the King of France. A large amount of supplies was found in both forts.

Monckton changed the name of Fort Beausejour to Fort Cumberland, in honor of the Royal Duke who won the victory at Culloden, and as it was a much better fort than the one on the south side of the Missiquash, the troops were ordered to remain at Fort Cumberland.

This fort stands in a commanding position on the south-west summit of the high ridge of upland that separates the Missiquash from the Aulac valley. It was a fort of five bastions, with casemates, and was capable of accommodating eight hundred men. It mounted thirty guns. After it fell into the hands of the English it was great improved. A stone magazine (a part of which is still standing) was built outside the southern embankment. The moat was excavated to a much greater depth. Of late years the place has been shamefully neglected. On account of its historic associations many yearly visit the "Old Fort," and efforts have been made to enclose the grounds and make them more presentable.

The Acadians were still to be dealt with. Whether they should remain in the country and in the possession of their lands depended entirely on whether they would take the oath of allegiance to the Crown of Great Britain. This one condition accepted, they would be guaranteed all the privileges and immunities of British subjects. They refused, and the Expulsion followed. It was a hard and cruel measure, but they had had forty years of grace, and those who had thus long borne with them now decided their day of grace had ended.

One hundred and fifty years have since passed, but we find the Acadians are still here and are exercising an influence in Canada that is felt in all its Provinces. They are British subjects now, however, and while they have not lost their love for the country from which they sprang, nor for the flag for which their ancestors sacrificed so much, they are ready to stand by the Empire of Britain in war as well as in peace.

# CHAPTER II

## THE NEW ENGLAND IMMIGRATION, 1755-1770

THE expulsion of 1755 left the population of old Acadia so depleted that the Governor and Council felt that something must be done at once to add to its numbers. The first move in this direction was to offer exceptional advantages to the New England soldiers, who constituted the largest part of the force at the taking of Beausejour, if they would remain in the country. Very few, however, accepted the offer, and as the unsettled state of the country between 1755 and 1760 was most unfavorable to immigration, but little progress was made till the next decade.

During these years wandering bands of Acadians and Indians harrassed (sic) the English, shooting and scalping whenever opportunity offered. At Bay Verte, in the spring of 1755, nine soldiers belonging to a party under Lieutenant Bowan, were shot and scalped while out getting wood for the fort. Colonel Scott, commandant at Cumberland, immediately sent two hundred of the New England men to Bay Verte with a sergeant and ten men of the regulars. The sergeant replaced the men who were killed, and caused three weeks' supply of wood to be laid in. Shortly after this one of the regulars was killed, and one of the New England men was taken prisoner. These men had strayed in the woods down as far as the Tantramar with these unfortunate results.

In 1759, Governor Lawrence wrote from Halifax to the Board of Trade that "five soldiers had been killed and scalped near Fort Cumberland, and that a provision vessel had been boarded by French and Indians in the Bay of Fundy and carried up the River Petitcodiac." The five men were ambushed and killed in Upper Point de Bute, near a bridge that crossed a ravine on the farm now owned by Amos Trueman.

Up to this time the government of Nova Scotia was vested in a governor and council. This year, 1758, it was decided by the Home Government to allow the Province a Legislative Assembly. The Assembly was to consist of twenty-two members, twelve to be elected by the Province at large, four for the township of Halifax, four for the township of Lunenburg, one for Dartmouth, one for Lawrencetown, one for Annapolis, and one for Cumberland. Fifty qualified electors would constitute a township. The township elections were to continue during two days, and those for the Province four days.

The Assembly met for the first time on October 2nd, 1758. Nineteen members were present. This makes the Legislature of Halifax the oldest in the Dominion of Canada. This year, also, Governor Lawrence issued his first proclamation inviting the New Englanders to come to Nova Scotia and settle on the vacated Acadian farms.

This proclamation created a great deal of interest and inquiry, and finally led to a considerable number of New England farmers settling in different parts of the Province, Chignecto getting a good share of them. The first proclamation had, however, to be supplemented by a second, in which full liberty of conscience and the right to worship as they pleased was secured to Protestants of all denominations. This guarantee was not included in Lawrence's first invitation to the New Englanders, and the descendants of the Puritans had not read in vain the history of the sacrifices made by their forefathers to worship in their own way.

In July, 1759, Edward Mott, representing a committee of agents from Connecticut, arrived at Halifax and was given a schooner to proceed to Chignecto, to examine that part of the Province with a view to settlement. Mr. Mott and his party returned some months later and suggested some changes in the proposed grants, which were conceded by the Government.

It was estimated at this time that two thousand families could be comfortably settled in the districts of Chignecto, Cobequid, Pisquid, Minas and Annapolis. This year (1759) persons in Connecticut and Rhode Island sent Major Dennison, Jonathan Harris, James Otis, James Fuller, and John Hicks, to Halifax to look out for desirable locations for settlement in the Province. Messrs. Hicks and Fuller decided to take up lands at Pisquid or Windsor.

From this time till 1766 the desire shown by residents of New England to settle in Nova Scotia was very marked, and resulted in adding considerably to the population of the Province.

In May, 1761, Captain Dogget was directed to bring twenty families and sixty head of cattle. The cattle were to be brought from the eastern part of New England to Liverpool, N.S., at the expense of the Government. Thirty-five pounds also was granted to transport twenty families with seventy-nine head of cattle to the township of Amherst. In 1763, a number of families came to Sackville and were given grants of land by the Government. These Sackville emigrants were adherents of the Baptist Church and brought their minister with them. The denomination is still strong in that locality. A number of these emigrants, however, returned at the beginning of the Revolutionary War, and others after the war was over.

The townships of Cumberland, Amherst, and Sackville were established in 1763. The township of Cumberland had an area of 100,800 acres. It included all the territory between the La Planche and Aulac Rivers, and extended east to Bay Verte and southwest to the Cumberland Basin. Old Beausejour, now Fort Cumberland, was within the township of Cumberland.

Amherst township is said to have had a population at this time of thirty families, and Cumberland of thirty-five families. The township of Cumberland of (sic) was given 18,800 acres of marsh, and Sackville had 1,200 cres of marsh and 8,700 acres of woodland.

In 1763, a number of the leading men in Cumberland met together and appointed a committee to draft a memorial to the Governor, asking the privilege of sending a representative to the Assembly at Halifax. The request was granted, and Joshua Winslow was chosen as the first representative of the township. Colonel Fry had previous to this time represented Cumberland in the Assembly, but he was not elected by the people. The following is the text of the memorial:

"To the Honourable Montague Wilmot, Esquire, Lieutenant-Governor and Commander-in-Chief of His Majesty's Province of Nova Scotia, and Colonel of one of His Majesty's regiments of foot, etc., etc., etc.

"The inhabitants of the town of Cumberland, in Nova Scotia, beg leave to congratulate Your Honour on your appointment by His Majesty to the chief command of this Province and in your safe arrival therein. Although remote from the Capital, and perhaps last in our addresses, yet we flatter ourselves not the least sincere in assuring Your Honour of the happiness we feel in finding ourselves under your government.

"It would give us particular satisfaction was it in your power to look upon ourselves in the same light with the other towns in the Province. But as we are yet destitute of that sanction which would put us on the same footing with our neighbours, we cannot help presuming upon the liberty of signifying to Your Honour our regret thereat, and praying that you will be pleased to permit the solution of our affairs to be laid before you, not doubting but upon a just representation thereof you will be pleased to think we are deserving in common with the other settlements of Your Honour's countenance and protection. We beg to rely on your goodness therein.

"By desire of the inhabitants,

"(Signers),

| | |
|---|---|
| John Huston (Ch.). | Elijah Ayer. |
| Wm. Allen. | Josiah Throop. |
| J. Winslow. | Jos. Morse. |
| Abel Richardson. | |

"CUMBERLAND, Nov. 1st, 1763."

Although thirty-five families had settled in Cumberland at this time, and six hundred acres of land had been cleared of timber, the larger part of the land was still held by the Government. Application was therefore made in this year by the following persons for grants of land in Cumberland:

GRANTEES' NAMES

| | |
|---|---|
| Joseph Morse. | Joshua Winslow. |
| Elijah Ayer. | Jesse Bent. |

Josiah Throop.

John Huston.

James Law.

Sara Jones.

Obediah Ayer.

William How.

Arch. Hinshelwood.

Samuel Danks.

Zebulon Roe.

Henry King.

Jonathan Cole.

Jonathan Eddy.

Alex. Huston.

Thomas Proctor.

William Allan.

Daniel Gooden.

Ebenezer Storer.

Benine Danks.

John Allan.

Charles Oulton.

David ————.

Daniel Earl.

Anthony Burk.

John Fillmore.

Samuel Raymond.

John Collins.

Thomas Clews.

Abel Richardson.

Winkworth Allen.

Liffy Chappell.

The Glebe.

The School.

Gamaliel Smethurst.

Sennacherib Martyn.

Abel Richardson.

William Best, Sr.

William Nesbit.

Windser Eager.

Gideon Gardner.

Thomas Dickson.

John King.

Joshua Best.

Elieu Gardner.

William Huston.

Simeon Charters.

Brook Watson.

Jonathan Gay.

Martin Peck.

John Walker.

Henry M. Bonnell.

Amos Fuller.

Samuel Gay.

Assell Danks.

Isaac Danks.

Ebenezer ————.

Robert Watson.

William Welch.

William Sutherland.

Nehemiah Ward.

Joseph Ayer.

William Milburn.

George Allen.

Jabez Chappell.

The Presbyterian Minister

Col. Joseph Morse was a native of Delham, Mass., and took an active part in the Seven Years' War. He lost heavily in the expedition against Oswego. In crossing the Atlantic he was captured by the French, and obtained a good taste of the quality of French dungeons in which his health became shattered. He was exchanged, after which he visited London and received many marks of personal favor at the hands of George II, amongst these a pension, and tracts of land in Virginia and Nova Scotia. His last days were spent in Fort Lawrence, where he settled after the expulsion of the French. He left one son, Alpheus, and a daughter, Olive. The former married Theodora, a sister of Col. Jonathan Crane the father of Hon. Wm. Crane; the latter married Col. Wm. Eddy, of Revolutionary fame, who was afterwards killed in the British attack on Machais, and the Fort Lawrence property inherited by his wife was escheated to the Crown. After Alpheus Morse's death his widow married Major How, an officer in Eddy's command. Upon the failure of the rebellion, Mrs. How and Mrs. Eddy fled to the United States. Alpheus Morse's sons were Alpheus, James, Joseph, Silas, and John. The two first lived in Cumberland, where their descendants are still found. Judge Morse and Dr. Morse, of Amherst, are sons of James. Joseph emigrated to Ohio, where his descendants now live. Silas married a sister of Judge Alexander Stewart, C.B. Among his descendants are Sir Charles Tupper's family, Rev. Richards (sic) Simmonds' family, and Charles Fullerton, K.C. John Morse married a daughter of Sheriff Charles Chandler, the father of Lieutenant-Governor Chandler. Among his descendants are the family of the late Judge Morse of Dalhousie, and the C. Milner family of Sackville. A daughter of Alpheus Morse married Judge Stewart. Among his descendants are Judge Townsend of Halifax, and Senator Dickey's family of Amherst.

There were three Ayers—Elijah, Obediah and Joseph—who came with the emigration of 1763 and settled in Sackville. Obediah joined the Eddy rebels in 1776, and was made a commodore by the Continental Congress after he left Cumberland. The Ayers in Sackville are descendants of these grantees.

Josiah Throop was an engineer in the British army. He surveyed the township of Cumberland, and Throop's plan is still referred to. His grant was in Upper Point de Bute, where some of his descendants still live. He represented the township in the Halifax Assembly in 1765.

There were three Hustons—John, William and Alexander. They lived near Fort Cumberland. The name occurs still in the county of Cumberland.

Joshua Winslow, as we have stated, was the first representative sent from Cumberland to the Legislature at Halifax, and was a member of the Winslow family, so distinguished in colonial history. He was engaged at Chignecto with Capt. Huston, in the commissary business. The latter in one of his trips to Boston picked up a waif in the person of Brook Watson, a young man who had had one of his legs bitten off by a shark in West-Indian waters. Watson was trained under Winslow, and the foundation of his success was hereby laid. General Joshua was Commissary-General of the British in Nova Scotia. He left Fort Cumberland in 1783. He was paymaster of the troops in Quebec in 1791 and died there ten years later. A grandson of his, a Mr. Trott, lives at Niagara Falls in a fine old colonial mansion full of treasures of the Colonial period, with many relics and personal effects of General Winslow.

The Bents were from New England. There were two brothers, John and Jesse. John settled in Amherst and Jesse in Fort Lawrence. There are a large number of their descendants in the country.

Gamaliel Smethurst represented the county of Cumberland at Halifax, in 1770. He returned to England and published a book in London, in 1774, describing a voyage from Nepisiquit to Cumberland. None of this name, so far as we know, now reside in the country.

Sennacherib Martyn was a captain in Winslow's expedition to capture Fort Beausejour. He brought with him to Westmoreland Point, as slaves, a negro family, to whom he afterwards gave their freedom, and gave them also his name (now spelled Martin). Captain Martyn married the widow Oulton and settled in Jolicure. He was godfather to George and Elizabeth, the children of Col. William Allan.

James Law was a commissary at the fort and a colonel of militia. He was a large property owner in Point de Bute on both sides of the ridge. Reverses of fortune came, and finally he died a parish charge.

Benoni Danks represented the county of Cumberland at the Halifax Assembly. Tradition says his death was caused by falling into the hold of a vessel. The Danks left the country about the year 1830.

Thomas Dickson was born in Dublin, and came to Connecticut when an infant. He married a Wethered.

The Kings were from New England. They settled in Fort Lawrence, and from there removed to different parts of the country.

Jonathan Cole lived on Cole's Island and gave his name to the place. He had two sons, Martin and Ebenezer, the former of whom settled at Rockport and the latter at Dorchester. The name is still in the county.

William Allan was a Scotchman who came to Halifax with the party that founded that place in 1749. He soon after came to Cumberland. John and Winkworth Allan were his sons. His grant was in Upper Point de Bute, where his son John lived when he was sheriff of Cumberland.

George Allan was a son of William Allan. He had a son George, and all the other Allans are the descendants of the first William. Winkworth Allan went back to England and became a rich merchant.

Brook Watson lived with his Uncle Huston for a time, and was employed by the Government to assist in the Expulsion. He afterwards left the country, going to London, where he was remarkably successful in business, and among other honors became Lord Mayor of the city.

Jonathan and Samuel Gay were brothers. Jonathan returned to New England, but Samuel remained in the country settling near the old Fort Beausejour. He was a very large man, measuring six feet six inches in height, and broad in proportion. Samuel was afterwards made a judge. It is said that Judge Gay's daughter Fanny was in Boston at the time of the sea duel between the *Shannon* and the *Chesapeake*, and was with the crowd that lined the shore awaiting the result. When the news came that the British had won, she threw up her bonnet and cheered for the victors, greatly to the annoyance of the Americans.

Daniel Gooden was a soldier in the British army, and after his discharge settled in Bay Verte, where numbers of his descendants still live.

Charles Oulton remained in Cumberland, and a large number of his descendants are still living in the county of Westmoreland.

David Burnham remained, and a number of his descendants lived in Sackville and Bay Verte for a good many years. The name has now disappeared.

John Fillmore was from New England, and settled in Jolicure. He had a large family of sons and they settled in different parts of the Province. The name is still in frequent evidence.

The descendants of Samuel Raymond live in King's County.

The two Chappells, Liffy and Jabez, settled in Bay Verte and Tidnish. The name is still common in these localities.

John Walker's grant was on Bay Verte Road, where the name was found until quite recently.

The Bonnells remained in the county for a time, but afterwards removed to King's County, where the name still exists.

Amos Fuller remained and the name is yet found in the county of Cumberland.

The Watsons settled in Fort Lawrence and were very successful in business. The Eddy rebels, under Commodore Ayer, sacked Mr. Watson's premises one night and took the old gentleman prisoner, compelling him to carry a keg of rum to the vessel for the benefit of the sailors.

William Welch remained in the country, and his descendants are still here.

The Wards were from New England, and remained in the country. Nehemiah lived in Sackville and kept a tavern near the Four Corners.

Simeon Charters was from New England and remained in the country. The name is still in the Province.

The Abel Richardson family came from New England. The Yorkshire family of Richardson, whose descendants are still in Sackville, did not settle there until some years later.

The Bests were a New England family and the name is still in the country.

William Nesbit remained and the name is now found in Albert County.

Archibald Hinshelwood left the country.

The Roe name is still in Cumberland.

William How was probably son of the How that was shot by the Indians under a flag of truce.

None of the Proctor family now remain in the county.

There is no information about any of the following grantees: Gideon Gardner, Sara Jones, Ebenezer Storer, Daniel Earl, Anthony Burk. Windser Eager was from Dumfries, Scotland.

It is a matter of surprise that so many names to be found in the lists of a hundred years ago have so completely disappeared.

A large number of families who came from New England at this time settled on the St. John River. They called their settlement Maugerville. The name Sunbury was subsequently given to the whole of the Province west of Cumberland County.

The Hon. Charles Burpee, of Sheffield, writes me that there were about two hundred families who at this time found homes along the river. Some of their names were: Perley, Barker, Burpee, Stickney, Smith, Wasson, Bridges, Upton, Palmer, Coy, Estey, Estabrooks, Pickard, Hayward, Nevers, Hartt, Kenney, Coburn, Plummer, Sage, Whitney, Quinton, Moore, McKeen, Jewett.

Simonds and White came to St. John some three or four years before the others. The Rev. Mr. Noble was there before the Revolution, but he did not come with the first settlers.

Largely through the influence of the Loyalists, in 1784, the Province of New Brunswick was set off from Nova Scotia, and the Missiquash River made the boundary between the two Provinces. This division cut the old township of Cumberland into two halves. Those who conducted the business for New Brunswick wanted the line at La Planche, or further east, while the Nova Scotians wanted it at the Aulac or further west. They compromised on the Missiquash.[2] This divi-

[2] The establishment of the Missiquash as the boundary between the two Provinces was eminently satisfactory to New Brunswick, but not so to Nova Scotia, as the latter Province at once vigorously protested against it, and did not seem inclined to give up agitating for a change. In 1792 the House of Assembly of Nova Scotia presented an address to the Lieutenant-Governor, in which they say "there is a very pressing necessity of an alteration in the division line, between this and the neighboring Province of New Brunswick." This agitation for a change in the boundary was kept up for several years, and in the correspondence, three other lines are suggested by Nova Scotia as being preferable to the one that had been already chosen.

The first of these was one from the head of the tide on the Petitcodiac to the head of the tide on the Restigouche River. A second from the head of the tide on the Memramcook by a certain magnetic line to the salt water of Cocagne Harbor, and the third by the course of the Aulac River to its head, and thence by a given compass line to the Gulf of St. Lawrence.

The present line was last surveyed by Alex. Munroe in 1859, under Commissioner James Steadman, Esq., acting for New Brunswick, and Joseph Avard, Esq., for Nova Scotia. The line is thus described by the Commissioners: Commencing at the mouth of the Missiquash River, in Cumberland Bay, and thence following the several courses of the said river to a post near Black Island, thence north fifty-four degrees, twenty-five minutes east, crossing the south end of Black Island, two hundred and eighty-eight chains to the south angle of Trenholm's Island, thence south thirty-seven degrees east, eighty-five chains and eight-two links to a post, thence south seventy-six degrees east, forty-six chains and twenty links to the portage, thence south sixty-five degrees, forty-five minutes east, three hundred and ninety-four chains and forty links to Tidnish Bridge, then following the several courses of said river, along its northern upward bank to its mouth, thence following the north-westerly channel to the deep water of the Bay water, giving to Nova Scotia the control of the navigable waters on Tidnish River.

Those wishing to get fuller information relating to this or any of the boundaries of

sion made some trouble in nomenclature and has puzzled a good many persons since that date. The part of the old township of Cumberland on the west of the Missiquash became the parish of Westmoreland, in the county of Westmoreland. Fort Cumberland was in this district, and between Fort Cumberland and the old township of Cumberland, and the still older county of Cumberland, which once embraced the present Westmoreland and Albert counties, and the present county of Cumberland in Nova Scotia, there was a good deal of confusion. A number of years passed before Cumberland Point came to be called Westmoreland Point.

The following facts are taken from the anniversary number of the *Chignecto Post*, 1895:

"On the 15th August, 1761, Captain Benoni Danks, Messrs. William Allan, Abeil Richardson, John Huston and John Oates were appointed to divide the forfeited lands in the township of Cumberland.

"On the 19th August of the same year Captain Winckworth Tonge, Joshua Winslow, John Huston, John Jencks, Joshua Sprague, Valentine Estabrooks and William Maxwell were appointed a committee to admit persons into the township of Sackville.

"The first town meeting, or meeting of the committee, for Sackville township, took place on 20th July, 1762. It was held at the house of Mrs. Charity Bishop, who kept an inn at Cumberland. There were present Captain John Huston, Doctor John Jencks, Joshua Sprague, Valentine Estabrooks, William Maxwell and Joshua Winslow. Captain Huston was made chairman and Ichabod Comstock clerk.

"The conditions and locations of the proposed new grant of Sackville were of the first interest to the newly arrived settlers, and the proceedings were largely taken up with settling such matters. It was resolved that a family of six, and seven head of cattle, should have one and a half shares, or 750 acres.

"At the next meeting, held on 31st August, Mr. Elijah Ayers' name appears as a committeeman.

"At a town meeting, held on 18th April, 1770, Robert Scott was appointed moderator and Robert Foster, clerk. They, with John Thomas, were appointed a committee to settle with the old committee for the survey of the lands."

About 1786, the inhabitants of Sackville made a return of the state of the settlement to the Government to show that if a proposed escheat was made it would be attended with great confusion, as but few of the grants had not been improved. The actual settlers at that date, as set forth in the return, appear to have been as follows:

LETTER A.

| | |
|---|---|
| Samuel Bellew. | John Peck. |
| Joseph Brown. | John Barns. |

New Brunswick, will find the subject treated exhaustively in a work just published, entitled "A Monograph of the Evolution of the Boundaries of the Province of New Brunswick," by William F. Ganong, M.A., Ph.D., from which the above facts are taken.

Samuel Rogers.

Ebenezer Burnham.

Samuel Saunders.

Simon Baisley.

Valentine Estabrooks.

Wm. Carnforth.

Andrew Kinnear.

Abial Peck.

James Jincks.

Nathaniel Shelding.

Eleazer Olney.

Job Archernard.

Nathan Mason.

Jonathan Burnham.

LETTER B.

Charles Dixon.

Gilbert Seaman.

John Richardson.

Joseph Read.

John Fawcett.

Wm. Carnforth.

George Bulmer.

John Wry.

Thomas Bowser.

Moses Delesdernier.

Joseph Delesdernier.

Daniel Tingley.

Michael Burk.

Wm. Laurence.

Samuel Seamans.

Ben Tower.

Joseph Tower.

Elijah Ayer.

Joseph Thompson.

John Thompson.

Mark Patton.

Eliphalet Read.

Nehemiah Ayer.

Josiah Tingley.

James Cole.

Jonathan Cole.

Hezekiah King.

Valentine Estabrooks.

LETTER C.

Wm. Estabrooks.

Gideon Smith.

Daniel Stone.

Patton Estabrooks.

Pickering Snowdon.

Thomas Potter.

Nehemiah Ward.

John Weldon.

John Fillmore.

Jos. C. Lamb.

John Grace.

Josiah Hicks.

Angus McPhee.

Joseph Sears.

Wm. Fawcett.

Benjamin Emmerson.

Jonathan Eddy.

Titus Thornton.

# CHAPTER III

## THE YORKSHIRE IMMIGRATION

YORKSHIRE is grouped as one of the six northern counties of England. Jackson Wray calls it "one of the bonniest of English shires." It has an area of 6,076 square miles, making it the largest county in England. Its present population is a trifle over three millions. A coast-line of one hundred miles gives its people a fine chance to look out on the North Sea. The old town of Hull is the largest shipping port. Scarboro, on the coast, is the great watering-place for the north of England. Leeds, Sheffield, Hull and Bradford are the largest towns. It is the principal seat of the woollen manufacture in Great Britain. The people are self-reliant and progressive. In Yorkshire to-day are to be found the oldest co-operative corn-mills and the oldest co-operative stores in England. The practice of dividing profits among purchasers in proportion to their trade at the store was first adopted by a Yorkshire society. This is just what might be expected from the people who, in 1793, passed the following resolution: "Resolved, that monopolies are inconsistent with the true principles of commerce, because they restrain at once the spirit of enterprise and the freedom of competition, and are injurious to the country where they exist, because the monopolist, by fixing the rate of both sale and purchase, can oppress the public at discretion."

Another resolution passed by the same corporation, but earlier in the century, shows our ancestors in a somewhat different light. A day of thanksgiving was appointed for the success of the British forces. The corporation attended divine service in the parish church, after which it was agreed to meet at Mrs. Owen's, "at five of the clock, to drink to His Majesty's health and further good success," the expense of the evening to be at the corporation's charge.

The old Yorkshire men liked a good, honest horse-race, and fox-hunting was a favorite sport with them. It is told of a Mr. Kirkton that he followed the hounds on horseback until he was eighty, and from that period to one hundred he regularly attended the unkennelling of the fox in his single chair. Scott's "Dandy Dinmont" could scarcely overtop that. No one can read the "Annals of Yorkshire" without being struck with the number of persons who at their death left bequests to the poor, widows getting a large share of this bounty.

John Wesley, very soon after he began his life-work, found his way to Yorkshire, and nowhere had he more sincere or devoted followers, many of whom were among the first emigrants to Nova Scotia. To the England of the eighteenth century America must have presented great attraction, especially to the tenant-farmer and the day-laborer. The farmer in that country could never hope to own his farm, and the wages of the agricultural laborer were so small that it was only by the strictest economy and the best of health that he could hope to escape the workhouse in his old age. In America land could be had for the asking. The continent was simply waiting for the hands of willing workers to make it the happy home of millions. The reaction in trade after the Seven Years' War made the prospect just starting in life gloomier than ever, and many a father and mother who expected to end their days in the Old Land, decided, for the sake of their children, to face the dangers of the western ocean and the trials of pioneer life.

Charles Dixon, one of the first of the Yorkshire emigrants, writes of England before he left: "I saw the troubles that were befalling my native country. Oppressions of every kind abounded, and it was very difficult to earn bread and keep a conscience void of offence." Under these circumstances, Mr. Dixon and a number of others decided to emigrate. It is not surprising then, that when Governor Franklin, at the invitation of the Duke of Rutland, went down to Yorkshire in 1771, to seek emigrants for Nova Scotia, he found a goodly number of persons ready to try their fortunes in the new land.

Governor Franklin did not stay long in the northern district, but left agents who, judging by the number that came to Nova Scotia during the few ensuing years, must have done their work well.

Among the first of the Yorkshire emigrants to sail for Nova Scotia was a party that left Liverpool in the good ship "*Duke of York*," on the 16th of March, 1772. The voyage lasted forty-six days, and at the end of that time the sixty-two passengers were all landed safely at Halifax. From that port they went by schooner to Chignecto, landing at Fort Cumberland on the 21st of May.

Charles Dixon, with his wife and four children, were passengers on the "*Duke of York*." Mr. Dixon's is the only record I have seen of this voyage, and it is very concise indeed. He writes: "We had a rough passage. None of us having been to sea before, much sea-sickness prevailed. At Halifax we were received with much joy by the gentlemen in general, but were much discouraged by others, and the account given us of Cumberland was enough to make the stoutest give way."

Mr. Dixon does not seem to have allowed these discouraging reports to influence him greatly, for by the 8th of June he had made a purchase of 2,500 acres of land in Sackville, and moved his family there.

Other vessels followed the "*Duke of York*" during 1773 and the two following years, the largest number coming in 1774. By May of that year, two brigantines moored at Halifax with 280 passengers, and three more vessels were expected. By the last of June nine passenger vessels had arrived. The ship *Adamant* at this time was the regular packet between Halifax and Great Britain.

As one of the passenger vessels was from Aberdeen, it is not likely that all the immigrants this year were from Yorkshire. At Halifax, the women and children going to Cumberland were put on board a schooner bound for Chignecto, and the younger man started to make the journey on foot. The latter took the usual road to Fort Edward; from there they went by boat to Parrsboro', and then followed the high ridge of land called the "Boar's Back," to River Hebert. At Minudie they found boats to carry them to Fort Cumberland, where they were given a right royal Yorkshire welcome by their wives and children, who had reached the fort before them. From Fort Cumberland the immigrants quickly began to look around the country for suitable locations.

Those by the name of Black, Freeze, Robinson, Lusby, Oxley and Forster bought farms at Amherst and Amherst Point. Keilor, Siddall, Wells, Lowerson, Trueman, Chapman, Donkin, Read, Carter, King, Trenholm, Dobson and Smith were the names of those who settled at Westmoreland Point, Point de Bute and Fort Lawrence. The names of the Sackville contingent were Dixon, Bowser, Atkinson, Anderson, Bulmer, Harper, Patterson, Fawcett, Richardson, Humphrey, Cornforth and Wry. Brown, Lodge, Ripley, Shepley, Pipes, Coates, Harrison, Fenwick and others settled at Nappan, Maccan and River Hebert.

Hants and King's County, in Nova Scotia, got a part of this immigration. Those who came to Cumberland were too late to secure any of the vacated Acadian farms before others had got possession, these lands having been pre-empted by the New Englanders and the traders who followed the army. Those who had the means, however, seem to have found no difficulty in purchasing from the owners, and very quickly set to work to adjust themselves to the new conditions. So effectually did they do this, that almost every man of them succeeded in making a comfortable home for his family.

The local historians of those times claim that these English settlers, arriving as they did just before the Revolutionary war, saved Nova Scotia to the British Crown. If that is the correct opinion, and we are more disposed to believe it is true than to question its accuracy, then the British Empire is more indebted to these loyal Yorkshire immigrants than history has ever given them credit for. The Eddy Rebellion proved that the New Englanders, who constituted a large part of the inhabitants of Chignecto previous to the arrival of the English, sympathized very generally with the revolutionists, and were ready to help their cause to the extent of taking up arms, if necessary, on its behalf. These English immigrants were not soldiers; most of them were farmers and mechanics who had taken little part in the discussions of public questions, but they were loyal subjects of the King of Great Britain. They always had been, and they always expected to be, loyal. The headquarters of the rebellion was in Cumberland, and it was in Cumberland that the largest number of these Englishmen settled.

In 1776, Mr. Arbuthnot writes, "There is an absolute necessity for troops to be sent to Fort Cumberland, Annapolis Royal, and a few to Fort Edward and Windsor for protection, with the help of His Majesty's loyal subjects who consist of English farmers. A sober, religious people, though ignorant of the use of arms, will afford every assistance." He says the others are from New England and will join in any rebellion. Murdock thinks that Arburthnot did not judge the New England men fairly; that many of them were loyal subjects of Great Britain, and did not want to be mixed up in the trouble and discussion between Great Britain and her older colonies.

Whether this English immigration did for Nova Scotia what is claimed for it or not, their success in the new country as farmers and settlers forever removed from the English mind the belief that Nova Scotia was a cold, barren and inhospitable country, "fit only as a home for convicts and Indians." And thus it opened the way for future settlers. It is not claiming too much to say these northern Englishmen were a superior class of men. Industrious, hardy, resourceful and God-fearing, they were made of the right material to form the groundwork of prosperous communities, and wherever this element predominated it was a guarantee that justice and order would be maintained. They were not all saints— perhaps none of them were—but there was a homely honesty and a fixedness of principle about the majority of them that "made for righteousness" wherever they were found.

The most considerable addition to the population of Nova Scotia after the Yorkshire immigration was in 1783 and 1784, when the United Empire Loyalists came to the Province. They left New England as the French left Acadia, without the choice of remaining. The story of their removal and bitter experiences has been told by more than one historian. They were the right stamp of men, and have left their impress on the provinces by the sea. Among the names of those who settled at the old Chignecto were: Fowler, Knapp, Palmer, Purdy, Pugsley. After the Loyalists there was no marked emigration to the Maritime Provinces till after the battle of Waterloo. The hard times in England following the war turned the attention of the people of Great Britain again to America, and from 1815 to 1830 there was a steady stream of emigrants, particularly from Scotland to the Provinces. Northern New Brunswick received a large share of these Scotch settlers. The Mains, Grahams, Girvins, McElmons, and the Braits of Galloway and Richibucto, in Kent County, and the Scotts, Murrays, Grants, and Blacklocks of Botsford, Westmoreland County, came at this time.

An account of the wreck of a ship in 1826, in the Gulf of St. Lawrence, is yet told by the descendants of some of those who were coming as settlers to Richibucto.

In the spring of 1826 a lumber vessel bound for Richibucto, N.B., carried a number of passengers for that part. When off the Magdalen Islands the vessel was stove in with the ice, and the crew and passengers had to take to the boats. There was no time to secure any provisions, and a little package of potato starch that a lady passenger had been using at the time of the accident, and carried with her, was the only thing eatable in the boats. Among the passengers was James Johnstone, of Dumfries, Scotland, and his daughter Jean, sixteen years old. For three days and nights the boats drifted. Mr. Johnstone, who was an old man, died from the cold and exposure, and at the time of his death his daughter was lying apparently unconscious in the bottom of one of the boats. On the morning of the fourth day a vessel bound for Miramichi discovered them and took all on board. After landing safely at Miramichi they took passage for Richibucto. Miss Johnstone married John Main of Richibucto, and was the mother of a large family. Mrs. Main was never able to overcome her dread of the sea after this dreadful experience.

The last immigrants who came to the vicinity of the Isthmus were from Ireland. They arrived in the decade between 1830 and 1840, and settled in a district now called Melrose. Until recently their settlement was known as the Emigrant Road. Some of the names of this immigration were: Lane, Carroll, Sweeney, Barry, Noonen, Mahoney and Hennessy. They proved good settlers, industrious and saving, and many of the second generation are filling prominent positions in the country. Ex-Warden Mahoney, of Melrose, and lawyers Sweeney and Riley, of Moncton, and Dr. Hennessy, of Bangor, Maine, are descended from this stock.

# CHAPTER IV
## THE EDDY REBELLION

THE Eddy Rebellion does not occupy much space in history, but it was an important event in the district where it occurred, and in the lives of those who were responsible for it. The leaders were Colonel Jonathan Eddy, Sheriff John Allan, or "Rebel John," as he was afterwards called, William Howe, and Samuel Rogers. Eddy, Rogers and Allan had been, or were at that time members of the Assembly at Halifax. Allan was a Scotsman by birth, the others were from New England.

The pretext for the rebellion was the militia order of Governor Legge; the real reason was the sympathy of the New Englanders with their brother colonists. It was represented at the Continental Congress that six hundred persons in Nova Scotia, whose names were given, were ready to join any army who might come to their help. If these six hundred names represented those who were of an age to bear arms, then the statement of Arbuthnot that the New Englanders were all disloyal was correct.

The first step taken in opposition to Governor Legge's order was to petition against its enforcement. The petition from Cumberland referred to the destruction of the fort on the St. John River as "rather an act of inconsideration than otherwise," and then said, "those of us who belong to New England, being invited into this Province by Governor Lawrence's proclamation, it must be the greatest piece of cruelty and imposition for them to be subjected to march into different parts in arms against their friends and relations. The Acadians among us being also under the same situation, most, if not all, having friends distributed in different parts of America, and that done by order of His Majesty."

This petition was signed by sixty-four persons in Cumberland, the Amherst petition was signed by fifty-eight, and the Sackville one by seventy-three. Fifty-one of the petitioners were Acadians. The date was December 23rd, 1775.

Governor Legge took no other action on these petitions than to send them at once to the British Government as evidence of the disloyalty of the Province, and at the same time he wrote to the Earl of Dartmouth that some persons had spread the report that he was trying to draw the militia to Halifax that he might transport them to New England and make soldiers of them. He also adds, "The consequence of such reports influenced the whole country, so that many companies of the militia have refused to assemble, ending in these remonstrances which here in a public manner have been transmitted to your Lordship."

As soon as it became known to the petitioners that Governor Legge would not cancel the militia order, and that the petitions had been forwarded to Downing Street, it was decided to elect delegates to meet in Cumberland to take into consideration what steps should next be taken. Accordingly, representatives appointed by the petitioners met at Inverma, the home of Sheriff Allan. Jonathan Eddy and Sheriff Allan were there as members of the convention, and took especial pains to urge upon the meeting that the time had arrived for decided action. Either they must cast in their lot with their friends in Massachusetts and Connecticut, or they must be loyal to the British Government. They also made it clear that they could not hold the country against the British without help from their friends. The decision must have been in favor of independent action, as almost immediately Colonel Eddy started for New England with the intention of securing help from that quarter. Allan remained for a while longer in the country, but his outspoken sympathy with the rebel cause was soon reported to the Government and steps were taken to have him arrested.

About this time Rogers' and Allan's seats in the Legislature were declared vacant, and a reward of two hundred pounds was offered for the apprehension of Eddy and one hundred pounds each for Allan, Rogers, and Howe. Allan's biographer, in writing of this period in his life, says, "His life being now in danger, he resolved to leave the Province for the revolted colonies; but previous to his departure he made several excursions among the Indians to the northward and by his influence secured for the rebel provinces the co-operation of a large number of the Micmac tribe." He left Cumberland in an open boat on August 3rd, 1776, and coasting along the Bay of Fundy, reached Passamaquoddy Bay on the 11th. In Machias Bay, which he entered on the 13th, he found Col. Eddy with twenty-eight others in a schooner on their way to the Bay of Fundy to capture Fort Cumberland. Allan tried to induce Eddy to abandon the expedition for the present, urging that it was impossible to accomplish anything with so small a force. Colonel Eddy was headstrong and sanguine, and kept on his way. He was sure more men would follow him, and he expected to get a large addition to his force when he reached the St. John River.

Allan, in the meantime, pushed on to Machias, and after spending a few days there, went as far as the Piscataquis River by water, and thence he took the stage to Boston. From Boston he proceeded to Washington's headquarters, giving New York, which was then in possession of the British, a wide berth. He dined with Washington, and talked over the situation. On the 4th of January he was introduced to the Continental Congress, where he made a full statement of matters in Nova Scotia.

After some deliberation, Congress appointed him Superintendent of the Eastern Indians and a colonel of infantry. He received his instructions from Hon. John Hancock, and left at once for Boston. While there he urged upon the members in council the necessity of protecting the eastern part of Maine, and showed the advantage it would be to the rebels if, by sending out an armed force, they could take possession of the western part of Nova Scotia. This the Council promised to do.

After giving this advice, Allan himself set out to show what could be done by raiding the loyal settlers on the River St. John. This expedition was not very successful, and Colonel Allan was glad to get back to Maine, and take up the duties of his new position as Superintendent of the Eastern Indians. He made Machias his headquarters, and to the end of his life, which came in the year 1805, he remained a resident of the State of Maine.

Beamish Murdoch, the historian of Nova Scotia, in a letter to a relative of Colonel John Allan, says: "If the traditions I have heard about John Allan are correct, he could not have been much over twenty-one years old in 1775. As he had no New England ancestors, his escapade must be attributed to ambition, romance, or pure zeal for what he thought was just and right. For the feelings against the Crown in Nova Scotia in 1775 were confined to the Acadian French, who resented the conquest, the Indians who were attached to them by habit and creed, and to the settlers who were emigrants from New England."

Mr. Murdoch was mistaken in the age of Allan. John Allan was born in Edinburgh Castle at about "half after one" of the clock, on January 3rd, 1746 (O. S.), and was baptized on the 5th by Mr. Glasgow. He thus must have been in his 30th year when he joined the Eddy rebels.

After Colonel Eddy's interview with Colonel Allan in Machias Bay, he pushed on to Cumberland, and landed in Petitcodiac. His little army had increased considerably since he left Machias. At the mouth of the Petitcodiac River he stationed a small force to watch for any reinforcements that might be coming to Fort Cumberland. With the main body of his followers he started overland for Chignecto, after he had supplied his commissariat from the loyal settlers along the river.

They crossed the Memramcook well up to the head of that river, and took a straight course for Point Midgic. Then going through the woods above the Jolicure Lakes, they came to the home of Colonel Allan, in Upper Point de Bute. Mrs. Allan and her children were still there, and there was no disposition on the part of the inhabitants of Jolicure to interfere in any measure against the rebels.

At Allan's it was learned that a vessel with provisions had been seen in the bay, heading for Fort Cumberland. Eddy sent a number of scouts down, with instructions to capture the vessel. Under the cover of darkness and a thick fog,they were able to locate the sloop in Cumberland Creek without being seen by the men on the look-out. In the early morning, when the leader of the scouts suddenly levelled his gun at the one man on deck, and called out, "If you move you are a dead man," the surprise was complete, and the man obeyed orders. The rebels boarded the sloop, and soon had all hands in irons. As it grew lighter, and the fog cleared away, Captain Baron and missionary Egleston from the fort came down to the vessel, suspecting nothing, and were both made prisoners. Egleston was taken to Boston, and remained a prisoner for eighteen months. As soon as the tide turned the vessel floated out of Cumberland Creek, and headed for the Missiquash. The Union Jack was hauled down and the Stars and Stripes run up in its place.

This capture greatly elated the rebels, furnishing them, as it did, with supplies, of which they probably stood in considerable need. The sloop could run up the Missiquash near to the farms of the Eddys, Jonathan and William, who at the time owned most of the upper part of Fort Lawrence.

Colonel Eddy now decided to lose no time, but attack the fort at once. His army camped at Mount Whatley, near where the residence of David Carter now stands. Mount Whatley was called Camp Hill for a number of years after this.

While these things were being done by the rebels the English were not idle. A hundred and fifty regulars, under Colonel Gorham, had been sent to assist the garrison and strengthen the defences of the fort. When all was ready in the rebel camp, Colonel Eddy sent the following summons to Lieutenant-Colonel Gorham, demanding his surrender:

> "To Joseph Gorham, Esq., Lieut.-Colonel Commandt. of the Royal Fencibles Americans, Commanding Fort Cumberland:
>
> "The already too plentiful Effusion of Human Blood in the Unhappy Contest between Great Britain and the Colonies, calls on every one engaged on either side, to use their utmost Efforts to prevent the Unnatural Carnage, but the Importance of the Cause on the side of America has made War necessary, and its Consequences, though in some Cases shocking, are yet unavoidable. But to Evidence that the Virtues of humanity are carefully attended to, to temper the Fortitude of a Soldier, I have to summon you in the Name of the United Colonies to surrender the Fort now under your Command, to the Army sent under me by the States of America. I do promise that if you surrender Yourselves as Prisoners of War you may depend upon being treated with the utmost Civility and Kind Treatment; if you refuse I am determined to storme the Fort, and you must abide the consequences.
>
> "Your answer is expected in four Hours after you receive this and the Flag to Return safe.
>
> > "I am Sir,
> > "Your most obedt. Hble. Servt.,
> > "JONA EDDY,
> > "Commanding Officer of the
> > United Forces.

"Nov. 10, 1776."

He received the following in reply:

> "FORT CUMBERLAND, 10th Nov., 1776.
>
> "SIR,
>
> "I acknowledge the receipt of a Letter (under coular of Flagg of Truce) Signed by one Jonan Eddy, Commanding officer, expressing a concern at the unhappy Contest at present Subsisting between Great Britain and the Colonys, and recommending those engaged on either side to use their Endeavors to prevent the too Plentiful effusion of human Blood, and further Summoning the Commanding officer to surrender this garrison. "From the Commencement of these Contest I have felt for my deluded Brother

Subjects and Countrymen of America, and for the many Innocent people they have wantonly Involved in the Horrors of an Unnatural Rebellion, and entertain every humane principle as well as an utter aversion to the Unnecessary effusion of Christian Blood. Therefore Command you in His Majesty's name to disarm yourself and party Immediately and Surrender to the King's Mercy, and further desire you would communicate the Inclosed Manifests to as many of the Inhabitants you can, and as Speedily as possible to prevent their being involved in the Same dangerous and Unhappy dilemma. "Be assured, Sir, I shall never dishonour the character of a Soldier by Surrendering my command to any Power except to that of my Sovereign from whence it originated. I am, Sir,

"Your most hble servt,
"Jos. GORHAM,
"Lt.-Col., Com'at, R. F. A.,
"Commanding Officer at Fort Cumberland."

The following is Colonel Eddy's own account of the first attack on Fort Cumberland, given in "Eastern Maine" (Kidder, p. 69): "Upon Colonel Gorham's Refusal to surrender we attempted to storm the Fort in the Night of the 12th Nov. with our scaling Ladders and other Accoutrements, but finding the Fort to be stronger than we imagined (occasioned by late Repairs), we thought fit to Relinquish our Design after a heavy firing from their Great Guns and small Arms, with Intermission for 2 Hours, which we Sustained without any Loss (except one Indian being wounded), who behaved very gallantly, and Retreated in good Order to our Camp."

Previous to the first attack on the place, Eddy had arranged with an Indian to sneak into the fort and open the main gate; he would have his men ready to rush in and take the place by assault. While the attack was in progress the Indian got into the place and was in the act of unbarring the gates when he was discovered by Major Dickson. The major spoiled the little scheme by slashing the Indian's arm with his sword, which left him maimed for life. The assailants soon after this retreated without any very serious loss.

In another attack, made a few days later, the large barracks on the south-east side of the fort were set on fire, in the hope that it would communicate with the magazine. It is said a traitor in the rebel camp warned the English of the second attack. This also failed, but the barracks and a number of houses near the fort were burned.

Before the rebels had a chance to make a third attack, a sloop of war arrived in the Basin with four hundred men to reinforce the garrison. Colonel Eddy seems not to have heard of the arrival of these troops. Their presence, however, enabled Col. Gorham to take the offensive, and the rebel camp was attacked. Eddy did not wait to try the mettle of his men, but got away with the loss of one man. With as many of his followers as he could hold together he hastened toward Bay Verte. A short distance beyond the Inverma Farm, a squad took ambush in a thicket near a bridge, and when the regulars in pursuit were crossing the bridge the party fired a volley, killing several of the soldiers and wounding others. This so incensed the troops that they returned and set fire to Sheriff Allan's house, which was burned to the ground, together with a number of other buildings in the neighborhood. Mrs. Allan and her children escaped to the woods, where they remained until hunger compelled them to come out. She was found some days after this by her father, Mark Patton, having lived for some time on baked potatoes picked up around the burned dwelling, and was taken to his home not far from the fort. Mrs. Allan was not allowed to remain long with her father, but was carried a prisoner to Halifax. She remained only in Halifax a few months when she was given her liberty and rejoined her husband at Machais.

Eddy, after going in the direction of Bay Verte for some time, finding he was not pursued, turned his steps toward Point Midgic, where he had called while on his march to Chignecto. From there he made his way back to Machais. Just what route he pursued, or how great the difficulties he met with in this long, tiresome journey, has never been given to the public. Machais, until the close of the war, was the rendezvous of privateers and all manner of adventurers, both before and after the arrival of Eddy and Allan. Colonel Eddy's escape from Chignecto ended the rebellion in that district so far as any hope remained of a successful attempt to hand over the government of the country to the New Englanders, but the differences of opinion among neighbors, the raids of rebel bands in the district, together with the burning of a number of buildings, created a strong feeling that it took years to allay.

Mr. James Dixon, in the "History of the Dixons," speaking of this period says:

"The rebels found more congenial employment in raiding the homes of the loyal and peaceable inhabitants, plundering them of such articles as they were in need of, and destroying or carrying away any guns or ammunition they might find. Mr. Dixon's home did not escape their unwelcome notice. His house was robbed of many valuable articles, some of which he kept for sale. For a considerable period the loyal inhabitants, notably the English settlers, were subjected to a state of anxiety, and lived in dread of a repetition of such unwelcome visits. On one occasion, when some of these people were approaching the house, Mrs. Dixon hastily gathered up her silverware and other valuables and deposited them in a barrel of pig feed, where they quite escaped the notice of the visitors. On a later occasion, when somewhat similar troublous times existed, Mr. Dixon, with the aid of his negro servant, Cleveland, hid his money and other valuables in the earth, binding his servant by a solemn oath never to divulge to anyone the place of concealment."

Nor was all the destruction of property chargeable to the rebels. At this time a number of the loyal settlers, who, it is said, had been drinking freely, surrounded the house of Mr. Obediah Ayer, who was in sympathy with the rebels, and set fire to his place, intending to burn the inmates. Mrs. Ayer was warned by her neighbors and escaped to the woods with her baby in her arms. After the raiders departed she with her children found a temporary home with a neighbor. Her husband did not dare appear for many days, but hid in the woods by day and visited his family at night.

The raid of Allan on the St. John gave the Government uneasiness in that quarter for some time longer. As mentioned before, there were two Eddys, Jonathan and William. They owned adjoining farms in Fort Lawrence. The upper road leading from Fort Lawrence to Amherst still bears the name of the "Eddy Road." It was probably made through the Eddy grant, and the Eddys may have been instrumental in its construction.

It is related that William Eddy, after the rebellion, came back to Fort Lawrence to settle his business and take his wife and family out of the country. To escape being made a prisoner at that time he kept hid in a hay-stack in the day-time and visited his home during the night. One night the soldiers who were watching saw him enter the house and at once surrounded the place, sending in two of their number to bring out the prisoner. Mrs. Eddy would give no knowledge of her husband's whereabouts. The house was thoroughly searched, but the man could not be found. The soldiers were dumbfounded. The fact is, that when Mrs. Eddy saw the soldiers coming, she told her husband to cover himself in a bin of grain in the chamber and place his mouth close to a crack on the side of the bin over which had been tacked a piece of list to prevent the grain from coming out. She would tear off the list and that would give him air to breathe. Her husband did as directed. When the officer who was making the search came to the grain-bin he thrust his sword into it, and said, "He is not there." Mr Eddy said afterwards that the sword went between his body and arm, so near was he being made a prisoner.

Inverma, the home of Sheriff Allan, is now owned, in part, by Councillor Amos Trueman, and is still called by that name. It consisted at that time of three hundred and forty-eight acres of marsh and upland and was no doubt part of the Allan grant of 1763. Besides the Sheriff's own house there were six or seven small houses occupied by Acadian families as tenants, also two large barns and four smaller ones.

Allan's wife was Mary Patton, the daughter of Mark Patton, who was at one time a large property-owner on the Isthmus. Patton Point, in the Missiquash valley, still goes by his name. His home farm joined the glebe lands of the parish, and was afterwards bought by William Trueman and given to his son, Thomas. I find the following entry in William Trueman's journal, referred to elsewhere:

"Old Mrs. Patton was buried at the burying-ground by Thomas Trueman, July 31st, in the 92nd year of her age."

This lady was no doubt Mrs. Allan's mother. She had continued to live at the old place after Thomas Trueman had taken possession, and as this was in the year 1808, she had lived thirty-two years after her daughter left the country.

The question has been asked, would it not have been better for the northern half of this continent if the Eddy rebellion had succeeded and what is now Canada had become one country with the United States? The name Americans could then fairly have been claimed by the citizens of the great Republic and a people whose interests and aspirations are identical, and whose religion, language and customs are the same, would have been united in carrying out the destiny of the Anglo-Saxon in America. This may sound very well, but events have transpired in the last hundred and twenty-five years that point unmistakably to the conclusion that the God of history intended this northern land called Canada to work out its own destiny independent of the southern Republic. At the period of the Eddy rebellion Nova Scotia was still in the cradle and had no grievances to redress. New Brunswick as a Province had no existence. Never in all history had a conquered country been treated so justly by the victors as had Quebec. Ontario at this time was but a western wilderness. It will thus be seen that there would have been no justification for the new settlers in this northern land to have joined hands with the thirteen older colonies.

Another preliminary objection can be found in the situation of the Loyalists of 1783, from the fact that one of the grandest band of exiles that was ever driven from fireside and country would have found no place on the continent to make new homes for themselves. This would have placed them in infinitely worse circumstances than that body of noble men and women of another race that twenty-eight years earlier in the century had been driven out as exiles to wander in hardship and want on that same New England coast. These Loyalists brought to Canada the sterling principle, the experience in local Government, the sturdy, independent manhood and business experience and energy which this northern land needed to make it one of the most prosperous and best governed countries in the world. To think what Canada would have been without the Loyalists helps one to see more clearly how fortunate it was that the Eddy rebellion was crushed.

The British Empire may owe more to the loyal Yorkshire emigrants than has ever been fairly accorded to them. Canada as a coterie of colonies furnished Great Britain with a training school for her statesmen that she did not otherwise possess. In this way British North America has been the prime factor in placing Great Britain first among the nations of the world in the government of colonies. It is true English ministers and English governors made mistakes and had much to learn before the present system was fully adopted, but the descendants of the Loyalists and those who remained true to the Crown during the stormy years of the Revolution were not likely to stir up strife without a just cause. And is it claiming too much to say that to Canada's remaining loyal in 1776 is due to a very large extent the proud position Great Britain holds to-day as the mother of nations, the founder of the greatest colonial empire the world has yet seen?

There are those who believe that the principle of equality and fraternity, of government by the people and for the people, the freedom for which the Pilgrim Fathers faced the stormy Atlantic and for which Washington fought against such odds, has been worked out in fuller measure and juster proportions in Canada than in the United States. Canada has helped greatly to emphasize the truth, only yet half understood by the world, that it makes little difference whether the chief ruler of a country is called president, king or emperor, or whether the government is called a monarchy or republic. These are but incidents. What is important, what is essential, if freedom is to be won and maintained, is that the people understand their rights and have the courage to maintain them at any sacrifice. It was the leaven of freedom working in the lump of the British people that gave the world the Magna Charta, Montford's rebellion, Cromwell and the Commonwealth, the Revolution of 1688, and the still greater Revolution of 1776.

This last event broke from the parent stem one of the strong branches of the Anglo-Saxon family, and gave each an opportunity to work out in different ways the ideals after which both were striving. And who will say that the descendants of Cromwellians and Quakers, Nonconformists and Churchmen, whose ancestors, from force of circumstances or love of country remained in their island home, are not to-day breathing the air of freedom as pure and unadulterated as their cousins on the banks of the Charles or in the valleys of the historic Brandywine. At any rate, we who live in this northern country, that escaped the cataclysm of 1776, feel that Canada has been no unimportant factor in helping to work out the great problem of government for and by the consent of the governed.

# CHAPTER V
## THE FIRST CHURCHES OF THE ISTHMUS

THE spiritual interests of the people of old Chignecto have always been well-looked after. One of the first white men to visit the Isthmus with a view to settlement was a priest, and the man who wielded the largest influence in and around Fort Beausejour during the last years of the French occupation was a priest, the vicar-general of Canada. In more than one instance the assistance promised to the colonists in Acadia by the wealthy was provisional upon the conversion of the Indians to Christianity. During the French period three chapels were erected on the Isthmus—one at the Four Corners, Tantramar, one at Fort Beausejour, and one at Beaubassin. These chapels were burned during the taking of Beausejour and the expulsion of the Acadians. The bell on the chapel at the Four Corners was buried by the Acadians at the intersection of two lines drawn from four springs to be seen in that locality yet. Some years after a party of Acadians, on getting the consent of Wm. Fawcett, who in the meantime had come into possession of the land, dug up the bell and carried it to Memramcook. The late Father Lefebre exchanged it for a larger one. It is believed that the bell from the Beausejour chapel is the one now used in St. Mark's church, Mount Whatley. This bell is ornamented with scrolls and fleur-de-lis and has the following inscription:

AD HONOREM DEI
FECIT F.M. GROS,
A ROCHEFORT,
1734.

The first Protestant ministers on the Isthmus were Episcopalians. Mr. Woods, a clergyman of that denomination, was at Fort Lawrence in 1752, 1754 and 1756. In 1759 Rev. Thos. Wilkinson was at Fort Cumberland, and in 1760 it is recorded that Joshua Tiffs baptized Winkworth Allan at the fort. Between that date and the arrival of Rev. John Egleson no record has been found. Mr. Egleson was born a Presbyterian, and was educated for that Church. He was ordained, but afterwards changed his views, and joined the Anglicans. He was reordained by the Bishop of London, and sent, in 1769, to Chignecto, by the Society for the Propagation of the Gospel in Foreign Parts.

Reference is made in another part of this book to Mr. Egleson's capture by the Eddy rebels in 1776. He seems to have been the first to take possession of the glebe lands of the parish, and the farm was for many years called the "Egleson farm." The parish register containing the earliest records has been lost or destroyed, so that from the arrival of Mr. Egleson down to 1794 very little is known of the local history of the denomination.

In 1794 a meeting was held on the 27th February, at or near Fort Cumberland, and the following business was transacted: "Messrs. Gay, Siddall and Brownell were appointed a committee to prepare plans for a church, to be erected at once on the town plot, and to obtain subscriptions." The new church was to be 46 feet long and 34 feet wide, with 19-foot posts. Messrs. Gay, McMonagle and McCardy to be the Building Committee. This is the old St. Mark's Church, that stood so long at Mount Whatley. The first list of subscribers were:

William Allen, £3, in pine lumber.
Samuel Gay, £3, in timber.
Ralph Siddall, £3, in timber.
Titus Knapp, £3, in drawing stone.
James Law, £3, in drawing stone.
Jerry Brownell, £1 10s., in timber.

The cost of the church, when finished, was £310. Of this amount the people subscribed £170. The Bishop of Nova Scotia gave £70, and there remained a debt of £70.

Having succeeded so well in building the church, a meeting was called, at the request of Rev. Mr. Willoughby, to provide a house for the clergyman. His request was granted, and in 1795, Mr. Milledge being then the resident minister, the church-wardens agreed to pay two-thirds of the amount of rent for the house in which he was living until the parsonage was built.

At a meeting of the vestrymen in 1796, the school lands of the parish were rented to Spiller Fillimore for £7 5s. These lands now bring an annual rental of $200. In 1810 the church-wardens of St. Mark's church were:

| | |
|---|---|
| Amos Fowler. | Samuel Gay. |
| James Ryan. | John Trenholm. |
| Harmon Trueman. | Chas. Oulton. |
| Samuel McCardy. | Jas. Hewson. |
| William Copp. | William Tingley. |
| Geo. Wells. | Thos. Trueman. |

Bill Chappell.

At a meeting held Nov. 2nd, 1818, it was resolved to take down the church and rebuild, making the width thirty feet. No reason is given for this strange proceeding. The contractors for the work were Wm. Jones, Henry Chapman, and Thos. Trenholm. This building stood until 1880, when a new building of more modern architecture was erected on the same site, where it stands to-day. The names of the clergymen who have been resident or had the oversight of the church in Westmoreland since 1752, as far as can be found, are given below:

| | |
|---|---|
| Mr. Wood, 1752-6. | J. W. D. Gray. |
| Thos. Wilkinson, 1759. | R. B. Wiggins, 1831. |
| Joshua Tiffs, 1760. | G. S. Jarvis. |
| John Egleson, 1769. | R. B. Wiggins. |
| Mr. Willoughby, 1794. | Geo. Townshend. |
| John Milledge, 1795. | Robert Donald |
| Mr. Perkins, 1805. | Richard Simonds. |
| Rev. C. Milner, 1822. | Chas. Lee. |

Donald Bliss, 1852-1902.

The following entries referring to church matters are from Mr. Wm. Trueman's Journal:

"July 26th, 1803—Rev. Mr. Gray preached at the church, from Proverbs 6 c., 3v., 'Humble thyself and make sure thy friend.'" Mr. Gray was probably a visiting clergyman.

"July, 1806, Oct. 16th—William Allan was buried at the church-yard at Camp Hill, attended by a large concourse of people. Mr. Milledge preached a sermon."

"December 25th, 1806 (Christmas Day)—Mr. Bamford preached at Stone Meeting House (Methodist), and after, Mr. Perkins administered the sacrament. The house was full of people."

As far as is known there was not a resident Episcopal clergyman in Amherst until 1823. Christ Church was erected that year on the county courthouse ground. In 1842, through the efforts of Canon Townshend, a new church was built on the present site. Rev. J. W. D. Gray was the first clergyman. The Rev. Canon Townshend came to Amherst in 1834, and held the rectorship until his death.

## METHODISTS.

A letter written from England to Mr. Wm. Trueman, Prospect, in 1776, asks if the adherents of the Methodist societies have any place of worship to go to, or do they meet among themselves according to the usual way of the Methodists. The reply would be that they met amongst themselves, as there is no record of a "meeting house" until some years later.

The Methodists of the early Yorkshire emigration at first met quietly at the home of one of their number for their services. In 1779 religious interest deepened, and a wide-spread revival began. Meetings were held, followed by encouraging results. Among the new converts was Wm. Black, of Amherst, afterwards Bishop Black. It is recorded that at a quarterly meeting held, in 1780, at Wm. Trueman's, Wm. Black received a great blessing, and although only a young man, he took from that time a prominent part in the meetings of the neighborhood. Three young men, Scurr, Wells, and Fawkender, agreed with Wm. Black to visit in turn, each Sabbath, the settlements of Prospect, Fort Lawrence, and Amherst. From 1780 until after the first Methodist Conference of the Maritime Provinces, in 1786, Wm.

Black had charge of the Cumberland Circuit, which included from Wallace (then Ramshag) to Petitcodiac, taking in Bay Verte and Cape Tormentine. In 1782 the membership of the circuit numbered eighty-two. In 1786 the first Conference was held at Halifax.

Shortly before Conference Mr. Black, with his family, moved to Halifax, leaving in his place, at Cumberland, Mr. Graudin, of New Jersey. Mr. Graudin was sent back to Cumberland by the Conference. He was assisted by John Black, of Amherst, brother of Wm. Black. In 1787 Mr. Graudin was removed and his place taken by Mr. James Mann. That year land was bought on which to build a chapel, and in 1788 the first Methodist church in Canada was built at Point de Bute. It stood somewhat back from the road in the present cemetery. The house was of stone, with a roof of thatch. The following is the deed of the property on which the house was built:

"This Indenture, made this eighteenth day of September, on thousand seven hundred and eighty-eight, and in the twenty-eighth year of His Majesty's reign, between William Chapman, of Point de Bute, of the one part, and the Rev. Mr. John Wesley, of London, of the other part, witnesseth, that in consideration of five shillings currency, by the said John Wesley to the said William Chapman, truly paid before the sealing and delivering hereof, the receipt whereof the said William Chapman doth hereby acknowledge and for divers other considerations him thereunto moving, the said William Chapman hath granted, bargained and sold, and by these presents doth bargain and sell unto the said John Wesley and his successors in the Methodist line forever, one acre of land, situated and lying in the County of Westmoreland, and Province of New Brunswick, bounding on the west on land belonging to James Law, Esq., and on the south on the main road leading from Fort Cumberland to the Bay Verte, together with all privileges to the said premises appertaining and all the profits thereof with the right, title and interest in Law and Equity, to have and to hold the said acre of land, to him the said John Wesly and his successors in the Methodist Line forever, and to be appropriated for a preaching House and burying-ground, and other conveniences that shall be judged necessary to accommodate the same under the inspection and direction of the general assistant or the preacher by Conference stationed on the Circuit, together with Wm. Wells, Thomas Watson, Esq., Richard Lowerison, George Falkinther, Wm. Trueman, jun., Stephen Read, and James Metcalf to be Trustees to act in concert, and those to be only Trustees as long as they adhere to the Doctrine and Discipline of the said John Wesley and his connection, and in case of death or failure of any of these particulars the preacher is to nominate one in his room. Furthermore, the said William Chapman, for himself, his heirs, executors and administrators, doth covenant to and with the said John Wesley and his successors, the before mentioned demised premises, against the lawful claim or demand of any person or persons whatsoever, to warrant and secure and defend by these presents, in witness whereof I have hereunto set my hand and seal. Bargained year before written.

"Signed, sealed and delivered, in presence of

JAMES LAW, WILLIAM CHAPMAN.
SALLY LAW, JANE CHAPMAN.
"JAMES WRAY, Missionary."

James Wray, and Englishman, ordained and sent out by Wesley, arrived in 1788. He was the first ordained Methodist minister in Cumberland. Previous to this the sacrament of the Lord's Supper was administered by the Episcopal clergyman. This same year Mr. Black, Mr. John Mann, and Mr. James Mann went to Philadelphia and were ordained. Mr. Mann and Mr. Wray were both on the Cumberland circuit for a year, and Mr. James Mann remained in charge until 1791, when he was followed by Mr. Whitehead. From 1793 until 1797 Mr. Early, Mr. John Black and Mr. Benjamin Wilson were each at times preaching in the Stone Chapel. Mr. Wilson was alone in 1798, and assisted by Mr. Cooper in 1799. In 1800 Joshua Marsden came out from England and was sent to the Cumberland circuit, where he labored for three years.

The following are from the journal before referred to:

"1802, May 9th—Mr. Marsden preached his farewell sermon at the Stone Meeting House.

"May 10th—Mr. Marsden set out for Conference."

Mr. Wm. Bennet followed Mr. Marsden, coming directly from England to Cumberland, arriving at Mr. Trueman's on June 26th.

"June 26th—Mr. Bennet arrived at our house and went to Tantramar."

"27th—Mr. Bennet preached his first sermon at Tantramar."

"July 8th—This day was appointed by the Government as a day of thanksgiving for the blessings of peace. Mr. Bennet preached at the Amherst Court-House from Romans 12 c. 1 v. to a crowded and attentive audience."

The church at this time was in a fairly good financial condition. Point de Bute was then headquarters for the ministers, it and Sackville being the most important places in the circuit. Mr. Mann visited Point de Bute in 1803, preaching at the Stone House on May 2nd, also June 16th.

"June 16th, Mr. Mann preached at Mr. Wells'."

"June 26th—Mr. Mann preached at the Stone House morning and evening to a crowded house."

Mr. Bennet's place was taken, in 1806, by Mr. Stephen Bamford, a local preacher sent out from England. he was afterwards ordained and remained three years.

"July 6th, 1806—Mr. Bamford preached at the Stone House for the first time."

On June 3rd, 1808, Mr. and Mrs. Wm. Black paid a visit to Point de Bute, making their home at Mr. Wm. Trueman's. It was a great joy to the church there to have Mr. Black with them again. In 1809-10-11, Mr. Knowlan was on the Cumberland Circuit, and in 1812 Mr. Bennet returned, followed by Mr. Dunbar, in 1815.

Mr. Dunbar remained three years and his place was taken by Mr. Priestly. During Mr. Priestly's stay the new church was built at Point de Bute. It stood in front of the spot occupied by the old Stone House, and was opened by Mr. Priestly in 1822.

Mr. Stephen Bamford was on the circuit 1823 to 1825; Wm. Temple in 1826 and 1827; Wm. Webb in 1828 and 1829; Wm. Smithson from 1830 to 1833.

In 1833, Rev. Alexander McLeod was sent to Cumberland as assistant. He made his home in Point de Bute, and was there most of the time until 1836. Rev. Richardson Douglas had charge of the circuit in 1834 and 1835. Mr. Jos. Bent came in 1836, and the house on the farm now owned by Mr. Burton Jones was rented for a parsonage. During Mr. Bent's ministry there was a large revival at Point de Bute, and about sixty members were received into the church. Mr. Bent was followed by Richard Williams, who remained two years. In 1840 the Sackville District was divided, the Point de Bute Circuit consisting of Point de Bute, Fort Lawrence, Bay Verte and Cape Tormentine. The Cumberland Circuit had been divided before this (as early as 1830), but the exact date cannot be found.

Below is a list of the ministers who have been resident in the Point de Bute Circuit since 1840:

> Wm. Leggit, 1840-1842.
> Geo. Millar, 1842-1843. Parsonage built.
> R. Williams, 1843-1844.
> Sampson Busby, 1844-1847.
> Wm. Smithson, 1847-1850.
> Geo. Johnson, 1850-1853.
> Wm. Smith, 1853-1856.
> T. H. Davies, 1856-1860.
> John Snowball, 1860-1861. Point de Bute Circuit again divided.
> Michael Pickles, 1861-1863.
> Chas. Stewart, 1863-1865.
> Geo. Butcher, 1865-1866.
> Robert Duncan, 1866-1868.
> Wm. Wilson, 1868-1870.
> Jas. G. Angwin, 1870-1873. Present parsonage built.
> Douglas Chapman, 1873-1876.
> Edwin Mills, 1876-1879.
> Geo. W. Fisher, 1879-1882. Present church built in 1881.
> Thos. Marshall, 1882-1884.
> W. W. Lodge, 1884-1885.
> S. R. Ackman, 1885-1888.
> Jas. Crisp, 1888-1891.

F. H. W. Pickles, 1891-1894.
J. A. Clark, 1894-1896.
T. L. Williams, 1896-1897.
Jos. Seller, 1897-1898.
D. Chapman, 1898-1901.
Thos. Marshall, 1901.

The first Methodist church in Sackville stood a little north of Philip Palmer's farm. It was opened in 1790 by Rev. James Mann. Previous to that date the preaching place had been a small schoolhouse, which stood near the place where J. L. Black's store now stands. The new building served its purpose for twenty-eight years. Then another was built at Crane's Corner, on the same site as the present church.

The following extracts from the Sackville Circuit Book of 1801-1811 may prove interesting:

## "QUARTERLY MEETING.

"Point De Bute, August 28th, 1802.

"(1) Q. Who is the general steward for the circuit? A. William Trueman. Elected.

"(2) Q. Who is steward for Sackville? A. John Fawcett. Elected.

"(3) Q. Who is steward for Dorchester? A. John Weldon. Elected.

"(4) Q. Who is steward for Amherst and the Rivers? A. Thomas Roach. Elected.

"(5) Q. How shall Mr. Bennett's expenses to New York be paid? A. Let it be approved by the next Conference.

"(6) Q. When and where shall the next quarterly meeting be held? A. At W. Fawcett's, Sackville, January 9th, 1803."

## "QUARTERLY MEETING.

"December 3rd, 1810.

"Q. Where shall a house be built for the circuit preacher? A. In Sackville, on the lands given by C. Dixon, Esq., and John Harris.

"Q. How shall the expenses be borne? A. By a subscription begun first in Sackville.

"Q. Of what material shall the said house be built? A. Of brick, except the cellar wall, which shall be made of stone.

"Q. Who shall be appointed to provide stone and timber during the winter previous to the next quarterly meeting? A. Charles Dixon and Rich. Bowser to see it provided out of the subscription. The said timber to be got for a house 34 by 24.

"Q. Shall the collections made in the Stone Chapel go to the discharging of the debt due to Mr. Trueman for the care of the said chapel? A. Yes, and also to the providing of wood for said chapel."

## "QUARTERLY MEETING.

"SACKVILLE, March 9th, 1811.

"*Q*. Shall the minutes of Dec. Q. M., 1810, respecting preacher's house be agreed to by this Q. M.? *A*. Yes, we are agreed that the house shall be built upon the grounds given by Messrs. Dixon and Harris.

"*Q*. Who shall be the trustees of the said house? *A*. John Fawcett, Jr., Chas. Dixon, Jr., Edwin Dixon, Esq., Rich. Bowser and Thomas Roach, Esq.

"*Q*. Who shall we employ to build the house? *A*. Chas. Dixon, Jr., who has engaged to finish it in a workmanlike manner for £200, according to plan, N. B., 35 ft. by 24, one story and half high and of brick."

## BAPTISTS.

In 1763 a Baptist church at Swansea, Mass., left in a body and settled in Sackville, bringing their pastor with them. They numbered thirteen members. Almost all of them returned to Massachusetts in 1771. The Baptists were the first Protestant denomination in Sackville, but had no church building until about the year 1800. That year Joseph Crandall organized the church, and they at once proceeded to erect a building in which to worship. The site chosen was at the Four Corners. The church which replaced this one in 1830 was called Beulah.

The first Baptist association for New Brunswick and Nova Scotia met in Sackville in 1810. Sackville was represented by Elders Jos. Crandall and Jonathan Cole, and by Messrs. Wm. Lawrence and Jos. Read. There were twenty-two elders and messengers present, representing fourteen churches. Amongst the representatives were Fathers Murray and Harding, and Peter Crandall, Nathan Cleveland and Elijah Estabrooks. A letter published in August, 1810, by Rev. David Merrill, in the *American Baptist Magazine*, reports his visit to the Association, in Sackville, as a member of the Lincoln Association, Maine. He is jubilant with hope for the new work and exclaims in triumph, "Babylon appears to be in full retreat." It is said that at a revival service in the Beulah Church, in 1822, conducted by Fathers Crandall, Tupper and McCully, twenty-five persons were immersed in Morris's millpond. During the service a woman stood up to exhort, handing her infant of six months to a bystander. The woman was Mrs. Tupper, and the infant the future Sir Charles Tupper. This must have been Sir Charles's first appearance in public life.

The Baptist Church in Amherst was organized about 1810, or perhaps a year or two earlier, by the Rev. Jos. Crandall. To the Association in Sackville they sent two messengers, Thos. S. Black and Wm. Freeman, reporting a membership of fifteen. The Rev. Chas. Tupper was the first pastor, ordained in 1817. He had charge of the church, with occasional relief, until 1851.

The Baptists of Westmoreland did not erect a church building until 1825. The late Wm. Tingley, of Point de Bute, gave the site and also the largest subscription. The following clause in the subscription paper is worth transcribing, as showing the liberality in religious matters which existed at that time. The Presbyterians of Jolicure assisted in the building, and were given "the right to hold service in proportion to the amount they subscribed, and when it is not in use by either Baptists or Presbyterians, if wanted occasionally by other denominations of Christians, it shall be open and free for such service." Although the building was erected in 1825 there was no church organized until 1850.

The first minister was Rev. Willard Parker, and the deacons Rufus Fillimore and Henry Ward. The ministers who have been in charge from that date down to the present time are:

| | |
|---|---|
| William Parker. | Trueman Bishop. |
| John Roe. Chas. | A. Eaton. |
| David Lawson. | T. D. Skinner. |
| W. A. Coleman. | J. D. Wilson. |
| G. F. Miles. | H. Lavers. |
| David McKeen. | D. A. Steele. |

## PRESBYTERIANS.

The Presbyterians were organized and had a church building in Amherst as early as 1788, but it was not until the Rev. Alexander Clark arrived, in 1827, that they had a regular minister stationed with them. Previous to this several ministers had been with them, but only a very short time.

In the grant of the Cumberland township of 1763 land was given to the Presbyterian Church on which to build a manse, but there is no existing record to show that it was ever taken possession of by that body. The first church in the township was erected in Jolicure about the year 1830. The land was given by Thos. Copp, and the Brownells and Copps of that place were very active in the work of building. Rev. Alexander Clark, of Amherst, was the minister in charge of the congregation. Dr. Clark spent his life in preaching the Gospel to the same people and to their children, with whom he began his mission when he first came to the country in 1827 or 1828. His circuit extended from Maccan to Pugwash, and from there along the Northumberland Straits to Shemogne, including Amherst, Jolicure, and Sackville. He was a fine type of the Scotch-Irish minister, who spoke what he believed was the truth, whatever the consequence might be.

## EPISCOPALIAN.

The first Episcopal Church in the Sackville Parish was built at Westcock in 1817. The rectors have been as follows:

John Burnyeot, 1818-1820.
Christopher Milner, 1820-1836.
John Black, 1836-1847.
T. DeWolfe, 1847-1860.
G. G. Roberts, 1860-1873.
David Nickerson, 1873-1875.
J. D. H. Brown, 1875-1878.

R. J. Uniacke, 1878-1879.
C. P. Mulvaney, 1879-1880.
C. F. Wiggins, 1880-

St. Paul's Church, Sackville, was commenced in 1856, and consecrated in 1858. The late Joseph F. Allison was largely instrumental in building this church. As the two churches, St. Paul's and St. Ann's, Westcock, were in the same parish, they were under the charge of one rector.

# CHAPTER VI
## THE TRUEMANS

WILLIAM TRUEMAN was born in Yorkshire, England, in the year 1720, and emigrated to America with his family in the year 1775. They were probably passengers in the ship *Jennie*, Captain Foster, which came to Halifax that spring with a number of emigrants from Yorkshire. The family consisted of William Trueman, his wife Ann, and their son William, an only child, a young man in his twenty-fourth year.

Billsdale[3] was the name of the township they left in the Old Country. They were Methodists in religion, but had been members of the Episcopal Church and brought with them the prayer-books and commentaries of that communion.

In addition to his business as a farmer, William Trueman, senior, had taken the legal steps necessary in England to enable him to work as a joiner if he were so inclined. The son William had been engaged in the dry goods business a year or two before coming to Nova Scotia.

After landing at Halifax they came by schooner to Fort Cumberland, and very soon after settled about four miles from the fort at Point de Bute, then called Prospect.

There does not seem to have been many of the name left in Yorkshire at this time, and those who were in Billsdale and vicinity shortly moved to other parts of the country. A nephew of the first William, named Harmon, moved to another township, married, and had a family of ten children. Mary, Harmon's youngest daughter, married a man named Brown, and they called one of their sons Trueman Brown. Charles, a son of Trueman, spent a year at Prospect in the eighties, and Harmon, a brother of Charles, visited the home in 1882-83. I have not been able to trace the family in Yorkshire in any but this one branch. There is a photograph at Prospect of John Trueman, a son of the Harmon here mentioned, which shows a strong likeness to some of the family in this country.

A family of Truemans living in Ontario came to Canada about the year 1850, but we have not been able to trace any relationship.

The first purchase of land by the Truemans in Nova Scotia was from Joshua

---

[3] Billsdale, Westside Township, is a long moorland township of widely scattered houses on the west side of the Rye, extending from six to eight miles N. N. W. from Helmsley, and is mainly the property of the Earl Haversham. Its area is 4,014 acres; its land rises on lofty fells at Rydale Head. Hawnby parish includes the five townships of Hawnby, Arden, Billsdale, Westside, Dale Town, and Snillsby, the area of the parish being 24,312 acres.

Mauger. This property was conveyed to William Trueman, sen. The deed reads: "I, Joshua Mauger, Esq., of London, in Great Britain, Esq. member of Parliament, of the town of Poole, in the county of Dorsetshire, for and in consideration of the sum of ninety pounds lawful money of the Province of Nova Scotia," etc., etc. This ninety pounds was paid for eighty acres of upland and fifty-four acres of marsh adjoining a wood lot on Bay Verte Road, and a right in the great division of woodland, so-called. The deed was signed at Halifax by the Hon. John Butler, as attorney for Joshua Mauger, on the 8th September, 1777, and the money paid the same day. Thomas Scurr and J. B. Dight were the witnesses, it was proved at Fort Cumberland on the 31st of Sept., 1777, by Thomas Scurr, and registered in New Brunswick by James Odell, May 3rd, 1785.

The next purchase of real estate was made from Thomas Scurr, the place now called Prospect Farm. Six hundred and fifty pounds lawful money of the Province of New Brunswick was the amount paid. Between the first and second purchase the Province had been divided, and that part of the township of Cumberland in which the Truemans settled had gone to New Brunswick. The number of acres in this last purchase was estimated at eight hundred, including nearly five hundred acres of wilderness land. The deed was witnessed by Thomas Chandler and Amos Botsford. Mrs. Scurr did not sign the deed, and the following is the copy of a document found very carefully laid away among the old papers at Prospect:

"VIRGINIA, PRINCESS ANN COUNTY,
"June 25th, 1789.

"On this day personally appeared before me, Dennis Dooley, Justice of the Peace of the said county of the commonwealth of Virginia, Elizabeth Scurr, and voluntarily relinquished her right of a dower in a certain tract or piece of land in the town of Westmoreland and Province of New Brunswick, viz.: Three eighty-acre lots, Nos. sixteen, eighteen and twenty, with the marsh and wilderness thereto belonging. All in division letter B, and described fully in a deed from Thomas Scurr to William Trueman and on record in Westmoreland, No. 142. "Given under my hand and seal this day as above.

"DENNIS DOOLEY.

"The within Elizabeth Scurr doth hereby voluntarily subscribe her name to the within contents.

"ELIZABETH SCURR."

Dennis Dooley, Justice of the Peace of the commonwealth of Virginia in the year 1789, was a good penman.

James Law owned Prospect Farm before Thomas Scurr. The deed conveying the property from Law to Scurr is still among the documents at Prospect. As Law was early in the country after the expulsion, it is probable he was the first to get possession after the removal of the Acadians.

Thomas Scurr, sen., left the country soon after selling Prospect Farm. The old chronicles say he was a man very much esteemed for his piety. He represented Cumberland township, for one session at least, in the Legislature at Halifax. In 1785, "in opposition to the advice of a friend against going from a place where was wanted to a place where he was not wanted," he removed to the South, and purchased an estate near Norfolk, Virginia. He repented too late, for nearly all the members of his large family fell victims to diseases peculiar to southern climates.

There was another Thomas Scurr in the country at this time, probably a son of Thomas Scurr, sen., who married Elizabeth Cornforth, of Sackville, in August, 1787. Mrs. Scurr lived only a week after giving birth to a son. The boy was called Benjamin, and was taken care of by his aunt, Mrs. Jonathan Burnham. Thomas Scurr, after the death of his wife, left Sackville with the intention of going to the West Indies, and was never heard from after. It was supposed he was lost at sea. The Scurrs in Sackville are descendants of the boy Benjamin.

William Trueman, sen., was above the average height, and rather stout, with head, shoulders and face that indicated strong character. In personal appearance his grandson Robert much resembled him. He was fifty-five years of age when he came to Nova Scotia. His wife was eight years his senior. She, too, was tall, with a countenance showing a great deal of reserve power.

William, the son, was a small man, with round features and dark hair. His son John was said to resemble him closely. He must have retained his youthful appearance well into mature life, for after he had been in this country some years he went to Fort Lawrence to poll his vote and was challenged for age by the opposing candidate. His youthful appearance had led to the belief that he had not arrived at the age to entitle him to exercise the franchise. His left arm was partially withered, or had not grown to its full size, from an injury received in childhood through the carelessness of a nurse. The family brought with them from England some furniture. There is still the old arm-chair at Prospect, and the old clock keeps good time for the fifth generation.

There is no record of the impression the new country made upon the family, but judging from a letter received by William Trueman, sen., the year after his arrival, and copied below, it must have been favorable:

"SNILLSWORTH, February 9th, 1776.

"DEAR BROTHER AND SISTER,—

"These are with our love to you and to let you know that we are in a tolerable state of health at present. "We have many of us been poorly, but are much better. We received a letter from you last November, which gave a great deal of satisfaction of mind on your account, because we had been informed that you had nowhere to settle in, but as you have given us a particular account concerning your situation and how you were settled and that you liked Nova Scotia and was all in good health of body it was much to our satisfaction, and I hope you will let us hear more particularly from you how your chattle and corn answers thee, and how and what product your ground doth bring forth, and what sort of grains your ground answers best for, and what chattle you keep, and what you can make of your chattle and how much milk your cows give and what is the most profitable things you have. "Now, dear brother, let me know the truth and nothing but the truth when you write. "I desire that you would let me hear from you at any opportunity whenever it suits your convenience for I think we shall never have the opportunity to see each other's face any more here below, but I desire to hear from thee and I hope thee will do the same by me as long as our lives shall be on this side eternity. "Farewell, I conclude with my love. Sarah Bently and John Bakers are in good health and send love to you all."

The following extract from another letter received at Prospect about the same time, will be interesting to some:

"SNILLSWORTH, Feb. 19th, 1776.

"DEAR BROTHER AND SISTER AND NEVY,—

"These are salutations of love to you all, expecting they may find you in good health as they leave us at present.

"We received your letter November last and was glad to hear from you, but more especially that you were all in good health of body and that you like 'Nove' (Nova Scotia) very well because we have had many slight accounts that you were in a very poor situation, but heard nothing to our satisfaction, and that you would have returned back to Old England but had nothing to pay your passage with, which gave us both me and my wife a great deal of distraction of mind. So we consulted with sister Sarah Bently and more of our friends that we would raise money to pay your passage to Old England, but dear brother and sister, as we have had a few lines from your own hand that you like the country well, so it has put and end to that consultation."

It would be difficult to answer at once some of the questions asked in these letters. They had only arrived in America the previous summer, and unless thy purchased cows on their arrival, they could not at this date have had much experience in dairying, and it would be the same with grain. There is a tradition that the stock, ten cows and a number of other cattle, were purchased with the Scurr farm, but this farm was not bought until some years after. The Truemans probably followed the course taken by many of the first settlers at that time, which was to lease a farm for a term of years, in that way gaining experience in the country before finally purchasing land themselves. After the family had been two years in the country, William Trueman, jun., married Elizabeth Keillor, a daughter of Thomas Keillor, of Cumberland Point, or No. 1, now called Fowler's Hill. The Keillors came from Skelton, Yorkshire, to Nova Scotia in 1774, and settled on the farm at present occupied by a great-great-grandson, Charles Fowler.

It was near the date of this marriage that the Eddy rebels were terrorizing the settlers around Fort Cumberland, and shortly after the event Mr. and Mrs. Trueman went to Mr. Keillor's to spend the Sabbath. During the day the house was surrounded by the rebels, and the inmates kept prisoners until the next day, when the rebels dispersed, and the young couple made their way home as quickly as possible, to relieve the anxiety at Prospect.

The Keillors and Truemans had been friends in England, and were related in some degree. Elizabeth Keillor was but nineteen when she consented to take charge of a home of her own, and, as subsequent years proved, well did she discharge the duties that devolved upon her in that relationship. Though below medium size, she had a nervous force and will-power that enabled her to accomplish more than many of stronger build. It is told of her that on a Sabbath, when the family were all at church, she noticed something wrong with the cattle, and on going to see what caused the trouble, she found a cow so badly injured by some of the larger animals, that to make the carcass of any value it would have to be slaughtered at once. Mrs. Trueman went to the house, got the butcher-knife, and bled the cow to death.

Nervous force, like any other force in man or woman, has its limit, and if used too fast it will not be there when wanted in old age. Mrs. Trueman did not live to be very old, and her last years were full of suffering. Overtaxed nature had given way, and the penalty had to be paid.

The family never separated, but all moved into the house on the Scurr farm, and began in earnest to face the battle of life in the New World.

Halifax was at that time the market for butter and beef, so after the wants of the settlers and the commissariat at Fort Cumberland had been supplied, such produce as could be sent by schooners to Halifax was forwarded in that way, and the cattle, for beef, were driven overland— a long and tedious journey.

Mills for sawing lumber or making flour were scarce. The stones are yet to be seen in Sackville with which grain was ground by hand-power.

The Truemans soon began to experiment in mill building. Their first venture was a mill driven by horse-power. A windmill followed, and was located on the high ground at the corner where the Point de Bute road turns at right angles, leading to Jolicure. This must have been an ideal spot for such a structure. There is no record of how long this mill stood, but it could not have been long.

There was a good stream on the farm for a water-mill, but it was not utilized for this purpose for some years, probably for the want of means. Their first work in this line was the building of a small mill on the brook that formed the ravine at the south-west side of the farm. A dam was thrown across the stream at the head of the ravine, and the water carried in a flume some distance farther down the brook; the great fall of water enabling them to use a large over-shot water-wheel. It is only quite recently that the main shaft of the wheel has disappeared.

A long dam was built across the stream that leads to what is now called the Upper Mill, for the purpose of turning the water to the new mill, and also forming a reserve pond. This dam can be plainly seen at the present time, although covered with quite a growth of timber. The mill in the ravine did not stand long either, and the next move was to dam the water on the main brook, now called the Trueman Mill Stream, and put up a large and substantial grist-mill, that proved a great convenience to the whole country for many years.

Beside this large expenditure in mills, most of which was made in the lifetime of the senior William, there was a large outlay made for dyking and aboideau building. Piece by piece the marsh was being reclaimed from the tide and made to yield its wealth of hay and pasture for the support of flocks and herds.

I find a record showing there were seventeen cows on the farm in 1790, and for the benefit of some of the members of the younger generation who live on farms, here are their names: Cerloo, Red-heifer, Spotty, Debro, Beauty, Madge, Lucy, Daisy, White-face, Mousie, Dun, Rose, Lady Cherry, Black-eye, Spunk and Roan.

The following letter, received at Prospect in 1789, tells of a more cheerful spirit in business in England, but shows that they had floods and troubles of that kind then as now:

"HELM HOUSE BILSDALE, Augt. ye 15th, 1789.

"DEAR COUSINS, —

"I received two letters from you in the course of the last year, and am exceeding glad to hear from you and that you do well and are well, and tho I have long delayed writing yet it is not want of respect, but it was long before I could have any certain inteligence from Mr. Swinburn, So I now take the oppertunity to let you know how I and my Sisters are situate. I married Helling the daughter of Richard Barr, by whom I have had 3 boys and 2 girls all liveing and healthfull. Aylsy is married to John the son of James Boyes and lives at Woolhousecroft, has no children. Sally is married to John Cossins and lives at Hawnby where Robt. Barker lived. She has 3 children the two last were twins they were born about Candlemas last and one of them is a very weakly child, my mother is married to old Rich'd Barr my wife's father and lives at Huntington nigh York. I think we most of us live pretty well. Mr. — —-has advanced his land a great deal but since the peace the times are pretty good we have this summer a very plentiful crop and we have a fine season for Reaping the same, but in the beginning of haytime we had an excessive flood as almost ever was known so that much hay was swept away and much more sanded. Many bridges were washed down and in some places much chattle drowned. My cousin John Garbut is married to James Boyes' widow and lives at Helm house. So I shall conclude with my and my wife's duty to my unkle and aunt and our kind love to you and your wife and children and subscribe ourselves your very affectionate cousins,

"JOHN AND HELLING TRUEMAN."

There was no break in the family by death until 1797. That year William Trueman, sen., died, aged seventy-seven years, twenty-two of which he had spent in America. The Mauger farm, his first purchase, was left to Harmon, his eldest grandson. The family of his son William had grown by this time to six sons and two daughters, and success financially, in some measure at least, had been achieved.

The "Brick House," Prospect Farm, erected 1799.

With milling, dyking and general farming, there was work at Prospect to keep all the members of the family busy, besides a large force of hired help.

It was decided this year (1797) to build a new house and barn, and the site fixed upon was about one hundred yards south of the Scurr house, where they had lived since the place came into their possession. The barn was put up the next year, and measured eighty feet long by thirty-three wide, with thirteen foot posts. A part of this barn is still used for a stable. In 1799 the house was built, the main portion being made of brick burned on the marsh near by. It fronted due south, and was twenty-seven feet by thirty-seven feet, and two stories high, with a stone kitchen on the west side. The cost of building was eight hundred pounds. This was before the days of stoves, there being six fire-places in the main house and large one in the kitchen.

In 1839 the stone kitchen was pulled down and one of wood built on the north side. In 1879 an addition was made, and now (October 2nd, 1900), it is as comfortable a dwelling as it has ever been. Five generations have lived in it. Three generations have been born and grown to manhood and womanhood within its four walls, and they have never known the death of a child, nor, with but one exception, the death of a young person.

On the 29th January, 1800, Mrs. Trueman, sen., died in the eighty-eighth year of her age. Although sixty-two years old when she came to America, she lived to see the birth of nine grandchildren.

In 1801, Thompson, the youngest son, was born. The family now numbered seven sons and three daughters. This year William Black, known in Methodist history as Bishop Black, was one of the family at Prospect from November 17th, 1801, to April 13th, 1802. One week of this time was spent in Dorchester, for which a rebate was made in the board bill. The bill was made out at the rate of five shillings per week.

In 1802, Mr. Trueman began to keep what he calls "a memorandum of events." The records chiefly refer to home work, the weather and neighborhood happenings. As a record of the weather, before thermometers and barometers were in general use, it must be as perfect as possible. As a record of farm work it is quite minute, and gives the reader an almost exact knowledge of what was done on the farm each week of the twenty years.

To those who live in the age of steam and electricity, when it is possible to be informed at night of the doings of the day on the other side of the planet, it is hard to realize how little interest was taken a century ago in anything outside of the community in which one lived. This accounts in part, no doubt, for the scant references in this journal to public events. Only very rarely is an election mentioned, even in the writer's own county. Only once is there reference to war, although the war of 1812 and the battle of Waterloo took place during the years of the record, and must have had a marked effect upon the trade of the Provinces at that time.

Mr. Trueman made several trips to Halifax each year, and met, while there, many of the leading Methodist men of the city. The Blacks and the Bells were his friends. His house was the home of the ministers of his church during all his life, and many of the public men who visited Cumberland were his guests at different times.

The first entry in the journal is dated May 5th, 1802, and reads: "wind N.W.; cold stormy day. Planted some apple trees; frost not out of the ground.

"May 6th—Wind N.W.; ground covered with snow two inches thick; disagreeable.

"May 8th—Wind N.W.; cold, backward weather. Mr. Marsdon preached his farewell sermon at the Stone Church."

"July 5th—This day was appointed by the Government as a day of thanksgiving for the blessings of peace. Mr. Bennet preached at Amherst Court House, from Psalm 12, 1st verse, to a crowded and very attentive audience.

"July 12th—Started for Halifax with thirty oxen. Returned on the 22nd; had a very good time."

(Ten days was the usual time taken on these trips. The drovers would start some hours, or perhaps a day, in advance of Mr. Trueman. He would go on horseback, in knee breeches, and with the old fashioned saddle-bags.)

"Sept. 28th—Started to Halifax with twenty-four cattle.

"Oct. 2nd—Arrived at Halifax Sunday night. Wm." (his son) "taken sick with measles. Monday, and Tuesday, very sick. Wednesday, some better. Thursday, walked the streets. Friday, started for home.

"Oct. 13th—High winds; very high tides; marshes much flooded.

"Sept. 14th, 1803—Stephen Millage died of shock of palsy. Mr. Oliphant, Methodist minister, arrived this month at our house.

"Nov. 12th, 1803—Election at Dorchester. Mr. Knapp goes in without opposition."

These extracts from the journal will show the character of the record.

In March, 1804, there was a three days' snowstorm—"fell nigh two feet." An attempt was made this year to aboideau the Aulac River, where it runs through the farm now owned by R. T. McLeod.

The Aulac at that time was one of the largest of the rivers emptying into the Cumberland Basin. It was a great undertaking to dam its waters with an aboideau, and to make matters worse, the place chosen proved to have a quicksand bottom, which made it almost impossible to build a firm foundation. For nearly four years they worked at this aboideau, and finally had to abandon it. Dated Dec. 27th, 1808, there is this entry in the journal: "Working at the aboideau. Storming in the morning. Snow six inches deep.

"Dec. 28th—Working at byto; very fine day. The hole nigh filled up."

On March 20th, he writes: "Concluded to give up the Byto." There is a reckless disregard of rules in spelling the word "aboideau," but doubtless the pronunciation was as varied then as now. Being obliged to let this work go must have been a great disappointment and a great loss as well. It was not till 1829, more than twenty years after, that the aboideau, now known as the "Trueman Byto," was built.

A night's experience during the building of the first aboideau was long remembered by the family at Prospect. The following is the only reference made to it in the journal: "June 7th, 1804—The sluice went adrift; was up to Nappan." On the 9th: "Got back as far as Cumberland; wind favorable in coming back."

The sluice referred to is a large wooden box or waterway, which is placed near the centre of the aboideau and as near as possible in the bed of the river. The great height of the tides, and the rapid current that runs up and down the stream twice in twenty-four hours, make it a most difficult operation to get one of these sluices bedded. The sluice would be about fifty feet long, fifteen feet wide, and five or six feet deep.

The men were hard at work after the sluice had been got into its place, trying to make it secure with the weight of mud, but the tide coming too quick for them lifted it out of its bed. Four of the Trueman boys sprang on the sluice as it floated down the river, in the hope of saving it in some way. It proved, however, to be a most unmanageable craft, and they could do little to stay their course down the river, and in spite of every effort were carried out into the Basin. Night came on and their only chance of safety was, if possible, to stick to the plank box in the hope that the currents might carry them to some point where they could get safely to shore. Next day their unwieldy craft grounded near Nappan, and they at once landed and were hospitably entertained at a farm-house near by. After getting supplies and sending word to Prospect of their safety, they again boarded their strange vessel and succeeded that day in getting back to the mouth of the river, and finally back to their starting point.

Mrs. Trueman never wholly recovered from the nervous shock of that night. There was little hope in the minds of any that the men would ever get safely to land.

Thirty years had passed since the family had left England. The letter given below shows how warm an interest the friends there still had in them:

"DEAR COUSIN,—We received yours dated Jan. 15, but not till late in September, 1804, and we are glad to hear that you and your family are all in good health and enjoying prosperity in your affairs of life. We had heard by your last letter of the death of your mother. My kind husband died something more than six years since. Your Aunt Sarah Bently died some time before my husband. Your Aunt Mary Flintoft is yet alive and enjoys as good health as can be expected, her age considered. Your Aunt Ann Trueman is yet alive and well as can be expected. Your Cousin Harmon married and is doing very well. He lives at Kelshaw, in the west of Yorkshire, and has a large family and keeps a public house. Alice is married and lives at Woodhouse Croft and has only one son. Ann and Sarah both live at Hornby and enjoy good health. I and my eight children live yet at the old habitation, namely at Helmhouse, and enjoy a sufficiency of the necessaries of life. Jane Chapman and Ann are both alive and enjoy as good health as most people at almost 80 years of age, and desire their kind love to you and your wife. James Hewgill and wife do the same. They never had any children. The last summer's crop of corn was poorly laden, so that wheat is now from ten to fifteen shillings per bushel, and is like to be more, as war being carried on makes taxes very high; but still, thanks to a kind Providence, industrious people may yet live above want. And soon shall all worldly calamities be over, and then if we are prepared for death we shall know woes and calamities no more. Pray write again when opportunity serves.

> "I remain your very loving cousin,
> "ELINOR TRUEMAN.

"Helmhouse, Billsdale.
"March 7th, 1805."

The first marriage in the family at Prospect was in July, 1805. The entry in the journal is: "Thomas and Mary were married by Rev. Mr. Perkins." Mr. Perkins was a minister of the Episcopal Church.

In 1806 I find this entry: "Mr. Bamford preached in the Stone Church, and Mr. Perkins administered the sacrament." This must have been before the Methodist minister was allowed to administer the sacrament.

Mr. Trueman was evidently mistaken in the name of Thomas's wife. He calls her Mary. Her name was Policene Gore; but as she was always called Polly, the mistake no doubt occurred in that way.

From a letter received from Rev. Wm. Black at this time, the following extract is taken:

> "I give you joy on the marriage of your son Thomas, and as I hear John is on the point of being married, too, I also wish you the same blessing on him. It would afford me much joy to hear that all your children were made acquainted with the saving benefits of religion. For parents to see their children well settled in this world and seeking the world to come must, I apprehend, be an unspeakable satisfaction. Oh, let us pray more and advise them to turn to the Lord with all their hearts. "Please to remember me kindly to all the family. I do feel a sincere regard for you all and wish to meet you in the Land of God.

> "Farewell,
> "From your unworthy friend,
> "WM. BLACK."

Policene Gore's mother had a more than ordinarily eventful life. Her grandson Edward writes:

> "My grandmother was born in the United States, then the New England colonies. Her first husband was Captain Ward; their

home was near the garrison on Grattan Heights. Captain Ward arrived home from sea with his vessel the day before Arnold made his attack on the garrison, and, joining in the defence, was fatally shot. Mrs. Ward's next husband was my grandfather Gore, who was also a sea-captain. Some years after they were married Captain Gore took his wife to Fort Lawrence, Nova Scotia, where they had friends, and her husband returned with his vessel to make another voyage, but was never heard from after. It was supposed the vessel was lost with all on board."

After living some years in widowhood, Mrs. Gore married a Mr. Foster, a school-teacher. They lived for a time in a house on the school lands in Jolicure. The schoolmaster did not live long to enjoy his married life. His successor was a Mr. Trites, of Salisbury. He only lived a few months after marriage. Mrs. Trites' fifth and last husband was a Mr. Siddall, of Westmoreland Point. After his death Mrs. Siddall lived with her daughter, Mrs. Trueman, where, in the words of her grandson, "she lived eighteen years, a happy old woman and a blessing in the family." She was in her eighty-fourth year at the time of her death.

Mrs. Siddall's house was the only one in the village not burned during the battle of Grattan's Heights. It is still kept in repair, and called the Gore House. Harmon, a grandson, visited the Heights a few years ago, and was present at the one-hundredth anniversary of the battle. Recently a letter came into the possession of Edward Trueman, written by his great-grandmother to his grandmother. Among other things, she writes: "I hear that you are married again, and that Policene is also married. I have not heard either of yours husbands' names; do write, and let me know them."

Policene Gore was born in 1788, and Thomas Trueman in 1786, which would make them seventeen and nineteen years old when the marriage knot was tied—a young couple to start out in life.

John married Nancy Palmer, September 12th, 1805, William married Jane Ripley, January 22nd, 1806, and Harmon, the first-born, married Cynthia Bent, June 8th, 1807. The four eldest sons were married within the year and a half, and on April 14th, 1808, Sallie, the eldest daughter, entered the matrimonial haven. This was thinning out the old home pretty fast. The sons, however, all settled near Prospect, and were several years getting finally located in their own homes. Harmon took the Mauger farm left him by his grandfather; Thomas, the Patten farm, joining the glebe. John settled at Mount Whatley; Willie took the mill property and farm now in possession of his grandsons, Amos and Johnston Trueman.

The drain on the home place to start for themselves so many of the family, and in so short a time, must have been considerable. Harmon had a house, and barn to build. Several entries in the journal refer to his getting out timber. On July 16th, 1806, Harmon raised his house. This house, yet one of the most comfortable in the place, is at present the property of A. C. Carter. Mrs. Carter is a granddaughter of Harmon.

April 22nd, 1806, I find this entry: "Robert Dickey and Nellie Chapman married. Started to frame the new mill."

"May 3rd—Saw mill and barn raised."

No mention is made of building a house for Willie, so probably there was one on the place. John and his wife lived for a time in the Scurr house, and for a time with Willie, before finally settling at Mount Whatley. Sallie married Gilbert Lawrence, of Westmoreland. It is said Sallie had an admirer who lived in Halifax, and occasionally visited Cumberland, and who in later years became a prominent official in the executive of that city.

In the early days and admirer a hundred miles distant was at a great disadvantage, and the "Fooler lad," as Sallie's mother called young Lawrence, won the prize.

Amos Fowler, of Westmoreland, or Fowler's Hill, married Miss Keillor, a sister of Mrs. Trueman. He was a Loyalist, and after living in this country some years, he visited the old home in New England, and on his return to New Brunswick brought with him his nephew, Gilbert Lawrence. After his marriage Gilbert settled at Amherst Point, and from there moved to Maccan, now called Southampton, where he was a very successful farmer for many years. He left the Maccan farm to a son a few years before his death, and bought a farm in Nappan. Here he spent the last years of his life, honored and respected for his sterling character.

# CHAPTER VII

## EXTRACTS FROM JOURNAL AND LETTERS

SOME extracts from the journal as a beginning to this chapter will, I hope, be interesting to some of the descendants:

"Aug. 2nd, 1802—Richard Lowerison's barn burned.

"Aug. 7th—Mr. Milledge preached at church. Got upland hay all up. Have 60 tons good hay in barn and in stock.

"Aug. 28th—Quarterly meeting at our house.

"Sept. 10th—Mr. Albro dined at our house." (Mr. Albro was a Halifax man who traded in cattle.)

"Dec. 28—John McCormick, apparently in good health, died instantly at night.

"May 10th—Mr. Marsden started to-day for the Conference.

"June 26th—Mr. Bent arrived at our house to-day and went over to Tantramar.

"June 27th—Mr. Bent preached his first sermon in Tantramar.

"May 3rd, 1803—William Bennet started for Conference.

"Dec.—Mrs. McMonagle's house was drawn from the plain to Mount Whatley.

"Jan. 9th, 1806—W. Wood Fillmore was married to Nancy Patterson, of Cole's Island.

"April 5th, 1806—Tolar Thompson brought a large birch log across the marsh on the ice, and also a load of grain to the mill and returned the next day.

"June 16th—Harmon had the old shop drawn to his house, had 17 yoke of oxen.

"William Allen was buried at the churchyard at Camp Hill, attended by a large concourse of people. Mr. Mitchell preached the sermon.

"Nov. 29th—Mr. Roach lost his vessel; the Capt. and two men were drowned; 515 firkins of butter saved.

"Jan. 12th, 1806—This day Wm. McKenzie was found dead, sitting in his chair, supposed to be frozen to death.

"June 3rd, 1808—Wm. Black came to our house and Mrs. Black and son, Martin Gay. Mr. Black preached at Stone Chapel.

In February of same year, "Mr. Foster came to mill in a cart and John Patterson from Cole's Island with a sled."

"Jan. 19th, 1808—Mr. Bamford moved to our house.

"Jan. 25th—A meeting to confer about the Byto[4]; nothing was done."

"Jan. 3rd, 1809—Martin Black married to Fanny Smith."

On the 8th of that month "William Black preached at Sackville, and on the 11th at Mr. Roach's in Lawrence; on the 16th William Black started for Halifax." "Feb. 23rd, 1809—Went to the Supreme Court. "Feb. 29th, 1810—Mrs. Roach, of Fort Lawrence, died to-day after a short sickness. Rev. Mr. Knowlton preached the funeral sermon from Psalms; a very solemn time; about five hundred people present. "In June, 1811, Robert Bryce purchased a lot of cattle and some butter in Cumberland. "June 28th—Went to Bay Verte with a drove of cattle and some sheep, put 32 cattle and 116 sheep on board vessel for Newfoundland. "July 8th— Started ten oxen for Halifax. John Trueman raising his house and barn, July 6th, 1811. "July 24th—Pulled the old mill down. A son of John Harper's was badly hurt at the mill brook."

I notice in the journal that "muster day" was in Sackville this year. It seems to have been a very prosperous year for the farmers of Cumberland. Shipments of cattle and sheep were made to Newfoundland and the usual supply sent to Halifax. The price paid must have been satisfactory; it would, at any rate, be so considered by our farmers now.

The following letter sent to Messrs. Reed and Albro, dated Sept. 6th, 1811, gives one an idea of the condition of the cattle trade at that time:

"WESTMORELAND, Sept. 6th, 1811.

"MESS. REED & ALBRO.

"Sir,—Recd. Your letter by Thomas Roach, Esq., respecting cattle; have been looking around for some cattle, cannot buy for less than 6d. (10c.). Mr. ——, of Westmoreland, has some good cattle unsold at present. If you wish me to purchase you some cattle you may depend on my doing the best in my power for you. Wishing your answer as soon as possible, as the good cattle may be picked up. I wish you would send me the weights of the different lots of Beeves. I cannot settle with the people I purchased from for want of the weights. Have given two drafts on you, one on Saml. Holsted for £200, payable on the 20th July, and one on A. Fowler for £100, payable on the 28th July. "You will oblige me much by calling on Wm. Allan and take up a mortgage deed belonging to Thomas King, of Westmoreland. "There is, he thinks, about £50 or a little more due on it. Send it to me and I shall get the money paid me on sight, as I want a letter. And in so doing you will much

---

[4] This, I suppose, was the aboideau that had to be abandoned, to which reference has been made.

"Oblige your well wisher,
"WM. TRUEMAN.

"P.S.—Thomas Roach, Esq., will furnish you with ten cattle at 6d, delivered in Halifax. If you accept his offer, send a boy to Windsor to meet the cattle. Please to write the first opportunity and inform me what I shall do. Do you want a few firkins of butter this fall? I have given Harmon Trueman an order on you bearing date of 7th Sept.

"I am your humble servant,
"WM. TRUEMAN."

The following letter, a copy of which is among the papers at Prospect, also adds some information about trade at that time:

"WESTMORELAND, March 7th, 1812.

"MR. JOHN ALBRO:

"Dear Sir,— I hope these lines will find you and Mrs. Albro and family enjoying health and every other blessing. I take this opportunity to inform you that I expect to have 12 or 14 oxen to dispose of this summer. I wish you to have the preference. If you wish to have them shall be glad to have a line from you by Mr. Gore, as also what you think the price will be.

"I want no more than the market price.
"Remain your humble servant,
"WM. TRUEMAN.

"N.B.—John Keillor, Esq., hath four good oxen he wishes you to have with mine. They are four fine oxen. They are likely to be good by July 15th."

In addition to the buyers from Halifax, Newfoundland was this year sending to Westmoreland for a part of its beef supply. The letter below refers to the trade with that colony:

"WESTMORELAND, 30 Oct., 1811.

"MESSRS. JOHN & ROBERT BRYNE,—

"I sent you a few lines Sept. 4th. Thinking it a chance whether you received it or no, I take the liberty to send you a second. I think it will be a great advantage to you to have some hay purchased and drawn to the place in winter. "If you wish to have any purchased I will do it for you, only let me know the quantity you wish to have. Cattle have been as low as 4 pence or 5 pence in the spring. It is uncertain what the price may be, but I see no prospect of them being very high, as there is great plenty of cattle in the country. Should you want any in the spring you can rely on my doing the best in my power to serve you.

"Remain your most humble servant,

"Wm. Trueman."

Mr. Bryne had been in Westmoreland that summer and purchased a drove of cattle and sheep, which were shipped on June 28th, as noted previously.

On April 25th, 1811, Mrs. Keillor, Mrs. Trueman's mother, who had been living at Prospect since 1806, died. Her husband, Thomas Keillor, a stonemason by trade, died some years earlier. There is at Prospect a copy of a power of attorney given by Mrs. Keillor to her "trusty friend," Stephen Emmerson, to act for her in collecting rents and selling claims in Skelton, England, in connection with the property owned by her late husband.

This document was copied by Amos Botsford and witnessed by Wm. Botsford and Henry Chapman, jun., and dated Oct. 30th, 1810.

Mrs. Keillor was buried on the old farm at Fowler's Hill beside her husband in a small burying-ground that was formerly surrounded by a stone wall, part of which is still standing.

Mrs. Keillor's maiden name was Mary Thomson. She and two other married sisters—Jane, the wife of John Carter, and Ann, the wife of William Trueman—came with the Yorkshire emigration. These sisters left one brother at least in England, as the letter following, in reply to one received from George Thomson, will show:

"Prospect, March 29th, 1811.

"Dear Uncle And Aunt,— Received your welcome letter of March 29th, and was glad to hear from you and of your wellfare, and hoping these lines will find you and yours enjoying the same blessings of health and happiness. "I have to tell you of the death of my mother-in-law. She departed this life April 22nd. Your sister Jane is very well at present. "The rest of your family are all well. If you see fit to come out in the spring your friends will be glad to see you. It will be best for you to get a lumber vessel if you can. There hath been two vessels from Hull and one from Newcastle this summer. Respecting goods and merchandise, lay in well for common clothing. Bring some home-made linens and checks. Ox-chains and horse-traces and bridles. Everything in wood will be expensive. "You ask what bills I propose. Good bills on Halifax answer, but nothing will answer like cash here, as it may be some trouble to get them cashed. Mechanics of all kinds are wanted. Carpenters, 7 shillings 6 pence per day. We pay 4s. and 4s. 6d. for making a pair of shoes. A good tailor is much wanted. We pay 6s. for shoeing a horse. Bring a few scythes of the best quality. Baie Verte is the best place to land at; if you cannot make that out, St. John or Halifax. There may be some difficulty in getting a passage from Halifax by water. Shall look out for a place for you with a house on it. "May the Lord direct you and prosper your undertaking. Give my best respects to George Swinburne and wife. Let him know my wife and my ten children and myself are well. "I have nothing more at present to write. May the Lord direct you in all your ways, so prays your affectionate nephew and niece,

"WM. AND ELIZABETH TRUEMAN."

Mr. George Thompson did not emigrate to Nova Scotia as he expected when he wrote to his uncle and aunt. The following letter, written by his son five years later, explains why:

"DURHAM, Sept., 1816.

"DEAR COUSINS,—You probably would think it very strange our not writing to you for so long a time, but I can assure you it was not for want of affection or respect, but merely inadvertence; and no doubt you would think it strange, after my father wrote to inform you he intended setting out for America, that he never went, but the principal reason was that on second consideration he thought himself too far advanced in years to undertake so long a voyage, and the rest of the family except myself were not very willing. Consequently he immediately after that took a large farm, which I had principally to manage, otherwise I would have gone at that time. However, it is my wish to set out next spring, and have not written to inform you it, in order that I may have your answer before that, stating all particulars of the country, and if there be a good prospect for me. There is also an acquaintance of mine, a threshing machine maker and cartwright, has a desire to accompany me; therefore be so good as to say what prospect there is for such a man as he is. "All my brothers and sisters are married and settled, and my father and mother are very well and now live by themselves, retired from farming. "Hoping you and all friends are well, I shall conclude with kindest love to all,

"And remain, dear cousin,
"Yours affectionately,
"GEORGE THOMPSON.

"P.S.—Have the goodness to write the first opportunity, and direct to me at

"Harbour House,
"DURHAM."

It is quite possible the above letter did not receive a reply. A good deal of trouble had been taken to send full information to the father, and five years were allowed to pass before any acknowledgement was made. At all events, there is no record of a letter being sent to the son, and it is certain he did not come to this country.

The subjoined communication helps to show the depressed condition in England at that period, and that many were looking to America in the hope of bettering their condition:

"May 14th, 1819.

"DEAR COUSIN,—I hope these lines will find you all well, as they us at present. We thank God for it. "I intend to come over to America this spring If it should please God, For the state of England are very bad, Land has got so very dear that a livelihood cannot be got in England, and the taxes that Government lays on are very heavy, till they reduce so many to a lower class that the land will hardly support the poor. I hope you are in a better situation in America.

"We understand in England that the States of America are very flourishing at present. I intend to set off to America the first of June. If it should please God that I should get over safe, I hope to get to your house as soon as I can. All your cousins are in good health at present. Thank God for it, and they wish to be remembered to you and all your family.

"So I remain your most obedient cousin,
"JAMES BOYES,
"of Bilsdale.

"N.B.—By the wishes of one of your cousins, of the name of Harman Wedgwood, a son of Benjamin Wedgwood, a tailor, he would like to hear from you. He thinks you will give him some information of your country.

"He wants to come to live in your country, and if you please to give him some intelligence of tailors' wages in your country.

"So he remains your most obedient cousin.
"HARMAN WEDGWOOD,
"Hawnby."

"N.B.—If you please to write to him you must direct as follows:

"'HARMAN WEDGWOOD,
"'Hawnby,

"'Near Helmsley, Blackmoor,
"'Yorkshire, England.'"

There was no change in the family at Prospect after Sallie's marriage in 1808 until 1817. On Jan. 17th of the latter year Robert married Eunice Bent, of Fort Lawrence, a sister of Harmon's wife, and in October Amos married Susanna Ripley, a sister of Willie's wife.

Robert settled on a farm adjoining the homestead. His house was not built until the summer following his marriage. James, his eldest child, was born 30th October, 1817, in the Brick House at Prospect Farm. Amos settled at the head of Amherst (now called Truemanville). The following letter, written by his youngest daughter, Mrs. Sarah Patterson, is very interesting, as giving some idea of the experiences of that time:

"When my father first came to live in the place now called Truemanville it was a dense forest. In summer the only road was a bridle path. In winter, when the snow was on the ground, they could drive a pair of oxen and a sled along the road. "The winter my father was married, as soon as there was enough snow and frost, he and one of his brothers and another man set out to build a house. "They loaded a sled with boards, doors and windows, and provided themselves with bedding and provisions to last till the house was finished. They then hitched the oxen to the sled and started on their twenty-mile journey and most of the way on a trackless path. "When they arrived at their journey's end, they erected a rude hut to live in and commenced building a house. They did not have to go far for timber—it was standing all around the site chosen for the house. "They built a very nice log house, 15 ft. by 18 ft. Their greatest trouble in building was, the stones were so frosty they could not split them. They had to kindle a huge fire of brushwood and warm the stones through, when they split finely. "After they had built the house they returned home, having been absent about three weeks. "My father and mother then moved to their new home, and father began to build a saw mill and grist mill. "Their nearest neighbors were one and a half miles distant, unless we count the bears and foxes, and they were far too sociable for anything like comfort. Sheep and cattle had to be folded every night for some years. "After father had built his grist mill he used to keep quite a number of hogs. In the fall of the year, when the beechnuts began to drop, the men used to drive them into the woods, where they would live and grow fat on the nuts. One evening when my mother was returning from a visit to one of the neighbors she heard a terrible squealing in the woods. She at once suspected that bruin designed to dine off one of the hogs. She hastened home to summon the men to the rescue, but darkness coming on they had to give up the chase. However, bruin did not get any pork that night; the music was too much for him, and piggie escaped with some bad scratches. "A short time after this, ominous squeaks were heard from the woods. The men armed themselves with pitchforks and ran to the rescue. What should they meet but one of my uncles coming with an ox-cart. The wooden axles had got very dry on the long, rough road, and as they neared my father's the sound as the wheels turned resembled very closely that made by a hog under the paws of bruin. "Imagine the way of travelling in those days! I have heard my father say there were only two carriages between Point de Bute and Truemanville. Their principal mode of travel was on horseback. My father and mother visited Grandfather Trueman's with their three children. Mother took the youngest on one horse, and father took the two older ones on another horse; and yet we often hear people talk of the 'good old times.' "My father was a man of generous disposition. The poor and needy always found him ready to sympathize and help them. He often supplied grain to them when there was no prospect of payment. He would say, 'A farmer can do without many things, but not without seed grain.' That reminds me of an incident I will tell you, of our Grandfather Trueman. About thirty-five years ago my mother was visiting at Stephen Oxley's, at Tidnish, where she met an old lady whose name I forget; but no matter. When she heard my mother's name she began talking about Grandfather Trueman. She said she would never forget his kindness to her in her younger days when she and her husband first came from the Old Country and began life among strangers in very straightened circumstances. After passing through a hard winter in which food had been very scarce they found themselves in the spring without any seed wheat or the means of buying any. "Her husband was almost in despair. She tried to cheer him up by telling him that if she went to Mr. Trueman she thought he would help them. So her husband agreed to let her try her chance, and she mounted a horse and set out for Prospect Farm. Just as she arrived there another woman came in and asked Mr. Trueman to sell her some wheat, telling him she had money to pay for it. Grandfather said he had very little wheat to sell but he could let her have a bushel or two. The old lady said her heart almost sank within her; she thought her case was hopeless. However, she told him she, too, had come for seed wheat, but she had no money nor the means of getting any at present, and they were entirely without seed. Grandfather turned to the other woman and said, 'You have money' go to Mr.— —- (a neighbor), you can get as much as you want, and I will give this woman the grain.' Oh, how glad she felt! Words were too poor to express her thanks, and she went home rejoicing. In after years, when Providence had favored her with a goodly share of this world's goods, she could not tell this experience without the tears running down her cheeks. How true it is, 'The memory of the just is blessed.'"

The following letter received from a son of Rev. William Black, is of some interest:

"HALIFAX, N.S.,
"27th Sept. 1819.

"MR. WILLIAM TRUEMAN,

"DEAR SIR,—Your favor of the 20th inst. is at hand, and in reply to it, as relates to the probable price of Butter, I would state it as my opinion that it is likely to command about 14d. A considerable quantity of Irish Butter has already arrived and more is expected. A number of firkins have this day been sold at public auction at 1s. per lb.,—the quality is said to be very fair. Please say to Mrs. Wells that I have received her letter of the 24th inst., and shall do as she requests. Mrs. Black and family are well, and join me in best regards to Mrs. Trueman, Yourself and Family.

> "Yrs. Truly,
> "M. G. BLACK."

After Amos and Robert left Prospect for homes of their own, the family remained unchanged until 1820. That year, Mary, the second daughter, married William Humphrey, of Sackville. William Humphrey was a carpenter by trade but shortly after his marriage bought a farm in Upper Maccan and went quite extensively into farming and milling.

The Humphreys were from Yorkshire, and after coming to America, settled first at Falmouth, Nova Scotia. After the death of Wm. Humphrey, sen., Mrs. Humphrey, following the advice of her friend, Charles Dixon, moved to Sackville with her family of five children, three sons and two daughters. James Dixon says of Mrs. Humphrey, in his history of the Dixons: "She was evidently a capable woman," and judging from the position her descendants have taken in the new country he was probably right in his estimate.

As I remember the second William Humphrey, he was a man of more than ordinary intelligence, one who looked closely at both sides of a question, and with whom every new undertaking was well thought out beforehand. He had no place for the man who wanted to make a show. He was, for the times, a large employer of labor, and his men did not readily leave his employ. He was possessed of strong religious convictions, but was by no means demonstrative in such matters. His children were given good educational opportunities. Two of his sons studied and graduated at colleges in the United States, and two others were students at the old Academy, at Sackville.

The following letter, written by William, one of the sons who was educated in the United States, to his cousin Ruth, will show how graduates of that day looked upon life:

> "NEW HAVEN, June 27th, 1853.

> "DEAR COUSIN,

> "Your very welcome letter came to hand in due time, for which I am exceedingly obliged, especially as many of my correspondents have been dilatory and others have given me up altogether. But they probably have as much reason to complain of me as I have of them. The truth is my studies so occupy my attention that I am too much inclined to forget my friends. The acquisition of a profession presents such an immensity of labor that it would seem to require a lifetime to become proficient, especially when the small amount of energy that I can command is brought to bear upon it. However, I am not disposed to find fault with the labor

so long as there is so much that is intensely interesting and I can make respectable progress towards the grand crisis of a student's life. "New Haven is equally as attractive as it was during my college life and I feel more at home here than in any other place in the United States during the present summer so far. I have become acquainted with the professional men of the city from whom I have received many favors and many of whom I hope to regard as my future friends. Through their influence I have had an opportunity of treating a number of patients, which is no small advantage to me in my studies. I confess I am so much attached to the city I should like to make it my home if it were practicable, but it is so much crowded with physicians that there is no room for me. In reply to your question as to what pleasure it afforded me to receive my diploma, I can very readily say that it was far from affording me anything like a thrill of pleasure to look back upon my acquirements. I rather felt as a tired traveller might be supposed to feel when, having exerted himself to reach the top of the first peak on a mountain, he has only secured a position where he can see Alpine peaks towering to the skies, which he must scale before his journey is ended. I very many times have felt as though I was not a particle wiser since I graduated than before I first left home, yet I suppose I may claim more than this for myself without being thought vain or arrogant, but what advantage either myself or others are to reap from it remains to be seen. I hope I am better prepared to spend the remainder of my life more profitably than I was before, with higher aims and in possession of greater capacity for enjoyment myself and of doing good to others. I cannot yet tell when I shall get my medical degree, yet if fortune favors and I get along with my studies pretty well, it will not be longer than fourteen months. I would like to arrange my plans to leave for home as soon as I get through, but it is so long beforehand that I do not think about it yet. "I shall have a short vacation of a few weeks, commencing with August 1st, when I should like to be at home, but I do not deem it best for me to go this summer. I shall probably go into the country 'round. I shall probably return to Philadelphia early in October and spend the winter there, which will end my residence in that city, unless I should remain longer to attend the hospital and see more practice than I could otherwise. "From the accounts I hear from home you still have need of doctors, for people continue to be sick and die. "Think you there will be any patronage for me? But your answer will probably depend upon my worthiness of it. "But I must hasten to close. I shall be happy to hear from you whenever you are disposed to write. "Kind regards to your mother, sisters and brothers.

"Very sincerely yours,
"William F. Humphrey.

"To:
"Miss Ruth Trueman,
"Point de Bute."

The Humphreys have not increased rapidly in this country. There were three brothers in the first family, William, John and Christopher. John never married. Christopher married, but had no family. William had four sons, and these, with their father and uncles, made seven of the name then living in the provinces. Since then these four boys have married, and two of their sons, yet the males of the name just number seven to-day; and, strange to say, have remained at that figure the most of the time for the last seventy years. At present there are living four great-grandsons, and three great-great-grandsons of the first William.

Dr. Humphrey graduated in regular course, received his medical degree, and settled in St. John, New Brunswick, where he worked up a good practice. His health, however, gave way, and he died a comparatively young man.

Mrs. Bishop, a daughter of William Humphrey, writes: —

"I do not remember hearing my parents say much about their early life. I remember my father saying he gave a doubloon to the man who married them. They moved to Maccan very shortly after they were married. When grandmother Humphrey died they went to the funeral on horseback (thirty miles), and took John with them, then a young babe. (The baby, John, was the late John A. Humphrey, of Moncton.) I have heard mother say she took me to her father's funeral when I was four months old, another long ride on horseback."

Mrs. Bishop is the only one of the family now living.

Returning to the family at Prospect, Betty, the youngest daughter, was married to George Glendenning, in 1823. Her name was to have been Elizabeth, but one day previous to the baptism the minister was at the house and asked Mrs. Trueman what baby's name was to be. She said, "Oh, I suppose it will be Betty," meaning to have her baptized Elizabeth, but to call her Betty for short. When the minister came to the baptism, he did not ask the name, but baptized the baby Betty. The mother did not feel very well pleased about it, but Betty it had to be.

George Glendenning, George Moffat and George Dickson, three Dumfrieshire farmers, came to America in the spring of 1820. They had talked the matter over during the long evenings of the previous winter, and finally determined to try their fortunes in the New World.

The agricultural distress that prevailed in Ireland at that time affected Scotland also, and the wages of farm laborers was only a shilling a day in harvest time. No doubt the love of adventure and a desire to see more of world also had something to do with the decision of the young men. Passages were secured on the ship *Abiona*, bound for Miramichi, at which port the young men were safely landed early in May. John Steele was also a passenger in this vessel. He went to Cumberland and settled on the gulf shore near Wallace. Rev. Dr. Steele, of Amherst, is a grandson of

John Steele. George Moffat also went to Cumberland, and settled at River Hebert. Beside managing a farm he did a large business in sending beef cattle to the Halifax market. Mr. Moffat was a fine, honest man, "a canny Scot," who was always as good as his word and expected others to be the same.

George Glendenning had a brother living in St. John, and after landing at Miramichi he went direct to that place, where he had a short visit. There was not much in the surroundings of St. John that was attractive to the eye of a Scotch farmer, so the young emigrant decided to try another locality. He turned his steps toward "Old Chignecto," a long, hard walk. He made several attempts to get work on the way, always without success. At a farmhouse in Dorchester he might have got employment, but did not like the appearance of things about the place. Before leaving Dorchester he had become much discouraged, and remembering his early training in a godly house, determined to ask direction and guidance from his Heavenly Father. And so, falling on his knees, he prayed that he might be directed in his way so that by another night he might find a place where work could be had. After this earnest prayer he started out with more heart, but in the long walk through the Dorchester woods to Sackville, then on the "Four Corners," no work was found, and so the marsh was crossed and Prospect Farm was reached just as it began to grow dark. He would try his fortune here. An old man answered his knock at the door and bade him, "Come in," but in answer to his request for work said, "No, I do not want a man, but you had better not go any further to-night; we will keep you here." In the morning the proprietor of Prospect reversed his decision of the night before and decided to give the young Scotchman a trial. The result was that he remained with the family for three years, and when he left took with him as his wife the youngest daughter.

Mr. Glendenning settled on a new farm in Amherst Head (now Truemanville), and soon became one of the most successful farmers of the district. John Glendenning, of Amherst, is his son, and Rev. George Glendenning, of Halifax, N.S., and Robert Glendenning, M.D., of Mass., U.S., are his grandsons.

# CHAPTER VIII
## PROSPECT FARM

THOMPSON TRUEMAN, the youngest member of the family, was married in March, 1823, to Mary Freeze. He was only twenty-two years old, and young looking for that age. He used to say in later life that he married at just the right time. His wife was a daughter of Samuel Freeze, of Upper Sussex, King's County. Her mother was Margaret Wells, daughter of Williams Wells, of Point de Bute.

The Freezes came from Yorkshire to Cumberland in the *Duke of York*, the first vessel that landed Yorkshire emigrants at Halifax. Charles Dixon, the founder of the Dixon name in Sackville, with his family, came out at this time. The Freeze family, when they arrived in Nova Scotia, consisted of William Freeze, sen., his son William, with his wife and two children. Wm. Freeze, sen., remained in this country only a short time. It was supposed the vessel in which he took passage for England was lost, as his family never heard of him again.

The son, William, was a mason by trade, but settled on a farm in Amherst Point, now occupied by the Keillor brothers. He remained in Cumberland until the first of the present century, and then removed to Sussex, King's Country, N.B. He had become rather discouraged in his efforts to reclaim the salt marsh, and came to the conclusion that it would never be of much value.

It is said that Mr. Freeze and his two sons started in a small boat for Kentucky. When they got as far as the mouth of the Petitcodiac River, they turned their boat up the stream, going with the tide to the head of the river. Leaving the boat, they plunged into the forest and tramped for some distance. At last they concluded they had lost their way and were not likely to reach Kentucky on that route. After some consultation, the father climbed to the top of a tall tree, and from this altitude the rich interval lands of the Upper Kennebecasis were full in view.

"There is a valley," said Mr. Freeze, "and there is where my bones are to be laid."

Here Mr. Freeze got a grant of nine hundred acres of land, enough to make farms for himself and his four sons. William, a son, was a great reader and student. He was very fond of mathematics, and it is said that sometimes when he and his boys would go to the field to hoe, he would take a stick and mark on the ground a mathematical figure, and then demonstrate it for the benefit of his boys. The dinner horn would sound, and no potatoes had been hoed that morning. John, another son, was a fine singer and took great pleasure in giving singing lessons to the young people in the neighborhood. The Freezes could all sing, and most of the men were handy with the mason's tools, which led some wag to say that the Freezes were all born with stone hammers in one hand and a note-book in the other. Charles, the fourth son, was a half-brother and inherited the home farm. Charles was a great reader and was very fond of history. He was eccentric in some ways and would take long journeys on foot.

He did not take kindly to railway travel, and his nephews liked to tell about his planning one day to go by rail instead of walking, but going to the station before the train arrived, he said he "couldn't be detained" and started away on foot.

There were two daughters. Miriam married Matthew Fenwick, of Maccan, N.S., who afterward moved to the Millstream, in King's County, and was the first to plant the Fenwick name in that county.

Mary was the wife of Thomas Black, of Amherst (brother of Bishop Black). They had a large family. The youngest son, Rev. A. B. Black, died in 1900. The history of the Blacks in this country was written by Cyrus, another member of the family.

Samuel, the eldest son of William Freeze, was married three times, and had a family of twenty-one children—seven by his first wife, Margaret Wells, of Point de Bute; eight by his second wife, Bethia Wager, of Dutch Valley; and six by his third wife, a Miss Scott of Petitcodiac. The first family were all daughters. The tenth child was the first son born. Mr. Freeze elected several times to represent King's County in the Legislature at Fredericton, and while attending to his duties there he was taken with the illness that ended in his death.

The following letter is among the old papers at the Prospect, written by Samuel Freeze shortly after Polly's marriage:

"Sussex, King's County,
"February 25th, 1824.

"Dear Son And Daughter,—

"I received yours, favored by Mr. Stockton, and am happy to hear that you are all well, with a small exception, such as human nature is subject to.

"I am sorry to hear that the crop of hay has failed so much the last season, which must be a great injury to that part of the country. I believe that we will make out with what hay we have. You speak of driving oxen to St. John. The southerly weather that we had about the 12th of this month has raised the water and ice to such an unusual height that it has swept almost all the publick bridges downstream in this parish, which cuts off our communication from St. John by sleigh or sled, in a great measure, or I would have written the butcher, and then could have probably given you a satisfactory answer; but it is not the case.

"Mr. R. Stockton informs me that you can get 4½d. at your own barn. I think that, as the road is, you had better sell them for the 4½ per lb., than to risk the St. John market, as there is but very little shipping in at present, and they get what they want from a less distance, and the butchers will take every advantage if they have not been contracted for. This is my opinion, but do as you think proper.

"I have set my hands to get out some timber this winter. I think about 150 tons of yellow pine and 50 of hackmatack, if the sledding continues three weeks longer. My crop of grain on my new farm did not answer my expectations, a great part of it was struck with the rust. I suppose I will get on the whole 16 acres something more than 100 bushels of grain, viz., wheat, buckwheat and rye. I have since exchanged it for an old farm (and pay 170 pounds) situate one mile below Matthew Fenwick's, formerly owned by Benj. Kierstead. It cuts 30 tons of English hay. The buildings are in tolerable repair. Susan Freeze talks of coming to see you shortly. Through the mercy of God I and wife and family are all as well as common.

"Dear children, from your loving father.

"SAMUEL FREEZE."

"MR. THOMPSON TRUEMAN,
Westmoreland:

"You will please accept of our love and impart it to our children and friends.

"If, hereafter, you have beef to sell, and wish to take advantage of the St. John market, let me know, and I will get a butcher's letter what he will do, and if that suits, you can drive your cattle, but I did not get your letter in time to get an answer and send it back to you by the first of March.

"S. F."

A son of Samuel Freeze was sheriff of the county of King's, N.B., for a quarter of a century, and a grandson is at present acting as deputy sheriff in that county.

Polly Freeze left her home in Sussex to take care of her grandmother in Point de Bute, and was married there. She had visited her before, making the journey of eighty miles on horseback, in company with a friend. A great part of the way was through the woods, with no road but a bridle-path for the horses.

Thompson brought his bride to Prospect on the 11th of March, 1823. The marriage certificate reads:

"I hereby certify that Thompson Trueman, Bachelor, and Mary Freeze, Spinster, both of Point de Bute, co'ty of Westmoreland, were married by license this eleventh day of March, in the year of our Lord, one thousand eight hundred and twenty-three by me,

"Chris'n Milner,
Missionary at Sackville.

"In the presence of:
"Joseph Avard,
"Wm. Trueman."

Rev. Mr. Bamford was the Methodist minister on the Sackville Circuit, which also included Point de Bute, but a Methodist minister had not the right, at that time, to solemnize marriage. In 1822, the year before Thompson was married, a Methodist minister, writing of the Trueman family, says:

"It consists of an old gentleman, his wife and ten children, eight of whom are married, making twenty souls. Of this number only two are not members of Society, and they live so far from the means that they cannot attend. Eighteen of the family, and for anything that can be seen to the contrary, the whole family, are doing well, both as to this world and that which is to come. Nearly all those who are in our Society meet in one class at their parents', who are just tottering into the grave ripe for eternity, and they have lately subscribed one hundred and fifty pounds towards the erection of a chapel in their neighborhood."

This chapel was erected that year, and used for a place of worship till 1881, when it was superseded by the present church, built at Point de Bute Corner in that year.

I find the following entry in the journal, dated Oct. 2nd, 1820: "Picking apples; had twenty-one grandchildren to dinner; picked about 100 bushels; very dry weather." The last entry is dated June 21st, 1824: "Apples trees in full bloom; fine growing weather."

The date when the apples trees were in bloom was scarcely ever omitted in the twenty years' record, and it varied from the fourth of June to the twenty-first, which was the extreme limit. There is scarcely any change noticeable in the hand-writing from the first entry to the last, and he would be seventy-two years of age when the last entry was made.

On April 22nd, 1825, Mrs. Trueman died, in the sixty-eighth year of her age. She had lived to see all of her ten children married and the birth of more than a score of grandchildren. The last years of her life were years of suffering. Her husband outlived her a year and a half, passing away on the 9th September, 1826, in his seventy-fifth year. William Trueman and Charles Oulton, of Jolicure, died at nearly the same hour, and both were laid away in the old burying-ground at Point-de-Bute.

Prospect Farm was left to Thompson. He has been managing it for some years, and the business was settled without much trouble. Little change was necessary, as all the other members of the family has been provided for. There were legacies to pay, of course. Ruth and Albert, Thompson's two eldest children, were born before their grandfather's death.

The routine life at Prospect for the next ten or twelve years was without much change. Two sons and two daughters were added to the family. There was sickness, but the doctor's visits were not frequent. Mr. Trueman suffered at times from acute rheumatism, often so severe could not turn himself in bed.

In 1829 another attempt was made to aboideau the Aulac River, and this time it was successful. What proved good ground was found less than a half mile below the place chosen in 1805. Work to the amount of £1,096 15s. 6d. in the construction of this aboideau is credited to the following persons. I do not know that this is the full cost of the work.

| | | | |
|---|---|---|---|
| Harmon Trueman | £311 | 14s. | 9d. |
| Joseph D. Wells | 142 | 3 | 5 |
| William Trueman | 104 | 7 | 5 |
| Robert K. Trueman | 202 | 7 | 9 |
| Thomas Trueman | 64 | 15 | 4 |
| Thompson Trueman | 110 | 6 | 10 |
| William Trenholm | 100 | 0 | 0 |
| William Hewson | 60 | 0 | 0 |

This aboideau was superseded in 1840 by the Etter aboideau, which was thrown across the Aulac about two miles nearer the mouth of the river. This latter work was very expense to maintain. The foundation in one place seemed to be resting on quicksand, and was constantly settling. In 1860 it was decided to abandon the structure and build a new one about two hundred yards higher up the river. Two years were taken to finish the new work, and in the meantime the old aboideau was kept in repair, which gave much better facilities for working at the new one.

When the Eastern Extension Railroad was constructed, a right of way was secured by the company over the new aboideau, and later, when the road came into the hands of the Dominion Government, an arrangement was made with the commissioners of the aboideau for maintaining the work that has proved very satisfactory to both the owners of the marsh and the Government.

In the decade between 1830 and 1840 the price of farm produce had dropped very much below what it was in the earlier years of the century. I find Hugh Hamel bought at Prospect 559 lbs. of butter for 9d., or 15c., per lb., and 1,198 lbs. of cheese for 6d., or 10c. The next year, 1834, a sale of cattle was made to George Oulton for 4d. per lb., weight estimated. In 1811 the same description of beef brought ten cents.

In 1839 Rev. Mr. Bennet was for some months member of the home at Prospect, and later Rev. Mr. Douglas and Mrs. Douglas and Rev. Mr. Barrett spent some time here in the order of their occupancy of the Point de Bute Circuit.

In 1840 an influenza, much like la grippe, passed through the country and caused a great many deaths. The family at Prospect were nearly all down with it at once, but all recovered.

The saddest visitation that ever came to this home was in the year 1845. On the evening of the 28th July death came a sudden and unexpected guest. The day had been fine, and farm work was going on as usual. Mr. Trueman had been at the grist mill all day. The family had gathered for supper, and a horse stood saddled at the door. There was to be a trustee meeting at the church that evening, and Mr. Trueman was on of its members. Supper over, he mounted his horse to ride to the church. Ten minutes had not passed when the horse was seen without a rider, and Mr. Trueman was found a short distance from the house, where he had fallen, to all appearance, dead. He was quickly carried in and medical aid summoned, but all was of no avail. It was a heavy blow. Mrs. Trueman could not look upon life the same afterwards, and she never recovered from the great sorrow. There were seven children, the eldest, Ruth, twenty-one years of age, and the youngest, Mary, eighteen months.

Thompson Trueman was in his forty-fifth year. He was a heavy man, quite different in build from his brothers. The writer was but eight years old at that time, and so has learned about him mainly from others. He seems to have made a great many friends, and was looked upon as an upright man. One who knew him well said, when he heard of his death, this passage of Scripture came to his mind: "Help, Lord, for the godly man ceaseth, and the faithful fail from among the children of men."

The years that followed were trying ones at Prospect. The blight that ruined the potato crop in 1846, and the loss of the wheat crop a few years later by the weavil, were felt more keenly because of the loss of the controlling mind. To give an idea of the financial loss, I may mention the fact that in 1843 two thousand bushels of potatoes were grown on the farm, and in 1847 not enough were grown to supply the table. In addition to the great failure in these two staple crops, at that time the price of beef, pork and butter went down to a very low point. A pair of oxen that would girth from six to six and a half feet could be bought for forty-five or fifty dollars. Pork went down to 4 and 4½ cents per lb., and butter to 12 ½ cents, or a York shilling. In one of the best settlements in Nova Scotia a majority of the farms were mortgaged to carry their owners over these hard years. Those who remember the period in New Brunswick history will not be inclined to complain to-day.

Samuel Davis, with the help of Mrs. Trueman, managed Prospect Farm until the sons were able to take charge. Mr. Davis was a most faithful and kind-hearted man, and is remembered with the liveliest feelings of gratitude by the writer for the numberless ways in which he tried to make up to him a father's loss.

It is doubtful if the saw-mill, which was built in 1843, was ever a paying investment.

In 1849 a stone kiln and machinery for making oatmeal were added to the mill property. The loss of the wheat crop had lead the Government of the Province to encourage the use of oatmeal by offering a bonus of £25 to anyone who would build an oat-mill. This led to the addition, and oats were made into meal for a large district of country for a good many years; but the expense of keeping the dam up, and the frequency with which it was carried away by the freshets, must have absorbed most of the profits of the business.

Up to this time agriculture had been the principal industry on the Isthmus. The farmer was the prominent man in the neighborhood, and the aim of every young man was to get a farm of his own. Now, however, there came a change. In 1848 gold was discovered in California, and in 1849 and the early 50's numbers of our young men left for the gold-fields. Then came the telegraph service, which called for bright, intelligent young men. Ever since that date agriculture has declined relatively in the Maritime Provinces. As the years went by the products of the western wheat-fields came into competition with the home-grown article, and the result was soon felt in the milling business here. Since 1872 the grist-mill at Prospect, with its three run of stones, and the saw-mill as well, have been allowed to go to decay.

In 1856 Hiram Thompson married Tryphena Black, of Prince Edward Island, and settled on the second farm north of the old place. Later he sold this farm and moved to Searletown, Prince Edward Island. In 1857, Eliza, the second daughter, married William Avard, of Shemogue.

In 1860, April 11th, Mrs. Trueman died, in the sixty-second year of her age, and after fifteen years of widowhood. She had a large circle of friends, and was always ready to help those who were in need. After her husband's death she kept up the family altar, and few mothers have been more earnest in looking after the moral and spiritual welfare of their children.

In 1863, Howard, the third son, married Agnes Johnstone, of Napan, Miramichi, and remained at the old home. In January, 1864, Margaret, the third daughter, was married to George M. Black, of Dorchester. The same year, in May, Mrs. Howard Trueman died. In July, 1867, Howard married Mary Jean Main, of Kingston, Kent County, daughter of John Main, of that place. Mary, the youngest daughter, was married to William Prescott, of Bay Verte, in 1873.

The following minutes of a meeting held at Prospect January 4th, 1875, will be of interest:

"The meeting was organized by the appointment of David Lawrence as Chairman, and Howard Trueman as Secretary.

"The chairman stated the object of the meeting was to take steps to celebrate in some fitting way the arrival of the first Trueman family in Nova Scotia, which took place just a hundred years ago.

"On motion of S. B. Trueman, seconded by Edward Trueman, Resolved, that there be a gathering of the Trueman descendants at the old homestead sometime during the summer of 1875.

"Moved by John A. Humphrey, and seconded by Martin Trueman, and carried, that a committee be appointed to carry out the above resolution, said committee to consist of representatives from each branch of the family.

"The following were named as a committee:

| | |
|---|---|
| "Martin Trueman. | "Edward Trueman. |
| Henry Trueman. | Benjamin Trueman. |
| Thompson Trueman. | John Glendenning. |
| David Lawrence. | R. T. McLeod. |
| Harman Humphrey. | Albert Trueman. |
| "Howard Trueman. | |

"It was also decided to number the descendants and have written out a short history or genealogy of the family; also to place a marble monument to make the last resting-place of those who first came to America."

The celebration was held at Prospect Farm on the 14th July, 1875, and took the form of an all-day picnic. A programme was given, consisting of music and addresses. The invitations were not confined to the immediate connection. Friends of the family were included. It was estimated that about five hundred were present, many coming from widely different points. The social intercourse was greatly enjoyed, and was looked upon as one of the best features of the reunion.

The following census of the family to day (1875) was given out at that Meeting:

| | Born | Dead. | Living. |
|---|---|---|---|
| MR. WILLIAM TRUEMAN (2ND), MARRIED TO ELIZABETH KEILLOR,1777- | | | |
| Children | 10 | 10 | 0 |
| HARMAN TRUEMAN'S FAMILY— | | | |
| Children | 10 | 5 | 5 |
| Grandchildren | 28 | 3 | 25 |
| Great-grandchildren | 23 | 3 | 20 |
| | 61 | 11 | 50 |
| WILLIAM TRUEMAN'S FAMILY— | | | |
| Children | 11 | 1 | 10 |
| Grandchildren | 72 | 23 | 49 |
| Great-grandchildren | 99 | 22 | 77 |
| | 182 | 46 | 136 |
| JOHN TRUEMAN'S FAMILY— | | | |
| Children | 10 | 3 | 7 |
| Grandchildren | 30 | 7 | 23 |
| Great-grandchildren | 2 | 0 | 2 |

|  | 42 | 10 | 32 |
|---|---|---|---|
| THOMAS TRUEMAN'S FAMILY— | | | |
| Children | 13 | 7 | 6 |
| Grandchildren | 52 | 12 | 40 |
| Great-grandchildren | 42 | 10 | 32 |
| | 107 | 29 | 78 |
| SARAH LAWRENCE'S FAMILY— | | | |
| Children | 11 | 3 | 8 |
| Grandchildren | 51 | 12 | 39 |
| Great-grandchildren | 51 | 7 | 44 |
| | 113 | 22 | 91 |
| AMOS TRUEMAN'S FAMILY— | | | |
| Children | 9 | 3 | 6 |
| Grandchildren | 47 | 4 | 43 |
| Great-grandchildren | 17 | 0 | 17 |
| | 73 | 7 | 66 |
| ROBERT TRUEMAN'S FAMILY— | | | |
| Children | 3 | 1 | 2 |
| Grandchildren | 8 | 3 | 5 |
| Great-grandchildren | 2 | 1 | 1 |
| | 13 | 5 | 8 |
| MARY A. HUMPHREY'S FAMILY— | | | |
| Children | 7 | 4 | 3 |
| Grandchildren | 20 | 3 | 17 |
| Great-grandchildren | 1 | 0 | 1 |
| | 28 | 7 | 21 |
| BETTY GLENDENNING'S FAMILY— | | | |
| Children | 6 | 3 | 3 |
| Grandchildren | 13 | 0 | 13 |
| Great-grandchildren | 1 | 0 | 1 |
| | 20 | 3 | 17 |
| THOMPSON TRUEMAN'S FAMILY— | | | |
| Children | 7 | 0 | 7 |
| Grandchildren | 18 | 1 | 17 |
| Great-grandchildren | 0 | 0 | 0 |
| | 25 | 1 | 24 |

Total in the ten families    664        141        523

### Religious Denominations

| Family of | Methodists | Baptists | Presbyterians | Episcopalians | Total |
|---|---|---|---|---|---|
| William Trueman | 78 | 24 | 22 | 12 | 136 |
| Thomas Trueman | 45 | 33 | .. | .. | 78 |
| John Trueman | 32 | .. | .. | .. | 32 |
| Harmon Trueman | 50 | .. | .. | .. | 50 |
| Mary Ann Humphrey | 15 | 6 | .. | .. | 21 |
| Betty Glendenning | 9 | .. | 8 | .. | 17 |
| Amos Trueman | 16 | .. | 50 | .. | 66 |
| Sarah Lawrence | 80 | .. | 11 | .. | 91 |
| Robert Trueman | 8 | .. | .. | .. | 8 |
| Thompson Trueman | 24 | .. | .. | .. | 24 |
| Total | 357 | 63 | 91 | 12 | 523 |

### Occupations

| Family of | Farm | Mech | Tele graph | Tin smith | Carp | Assay | Teach | Student AtLaw | Rail | Own Mill | Agt |
|---|---|---|---|---|---|---|---|---|---|---|---|
| William Trueman | 16 | 1 | 1 | 1 | 3 | 1 | 1 | .. | .. | .. | .. |
| Thomas Trueman | 6 | 7 | .. | .. | 2 | .. | 1 | 1 | .. | .. | .. |
| John Trueman | 1 | .. | .. | .. | 1 | .. | .. | .. | .. | .. | .. |
| Harmon Trueman | 3 | 3 | .. | .. | 2 | .. | 1 | .. | 1 | .. | .. |
| Mary A. Humphrey | 1 | .. | .. | .. | .. | .. | 1 | .. | .. | 1 | .. |
| Betty Glendenning | 1 | .. | .. | .. | .. | .. | .. | .. | .. | .. | .. |
| Amos Trueman | 8 | .. | .. | .. | .. | .. | .. | .. | .. | .. | .. |
| Sarah Lawrence | 6 | 3 | .. | .. | .. | .. | 1 | .. | .. | .. | 1 |
| Robert Trueman | 1 | 1 | .. | .. | .. | .. | .. | .. | .. | .. | .. |
| Thompson Trueman | 3 | .. | .. | .. | .. | .. | .. | .. | .. | .. | .. |
| Total | 46 | 15 | 1 | 1 | 8 | 1 | 5 | 1 | 1 | 1 | 1 |

So much was this celebration enjoyed that the decision was quite unanimous that a similar reunion should be held at a future time. This was kept in mind, and in 1891, seventeen years afterwards, invitations were sent from Prospect for another gathering of the clan. This time, however, the scope of the celebration was extended. The Historical Society of Sackville was associated in the event, and all were welcome who cared to be present.

This gathering was called the Yorkshire Picnic, and anyone of Yorkshire blood was especially welcome. An effort was made to get the names of all visitors recorded, but it was not entirely successful. About three hundred, however, wrote their names below the following, written by Judge Morse.

"Visitors to Prospect Farm, July 14th, 1891, on the occasion of the reunion of the Trueman family, combined with a picnic of the Historical Society of Sackville, in commemoration of the coming into the country of the Yorkshire settlers,

"WILLIAM A. D. MORSE,
"Judge County Court,
"Nova Scotia."

The following is a report of that gathering as given in the Chignecto *Post* at that time:

"YORKSHIRE PICNIC.

"A LARGE GATHERING AT PROSPECT FARM—A SUCCESSFUL HISTORICAL MEETING.

"On Tuesday last, in response to invitations, upwards of five hundred persons gathered at Prospect Farm, Point de Bute, the residence of Messrs. Howard and Albert Trueman, to commemorate the arrival of the Yorkshire settlers in this country. The descendants of the Yorkshiremen had invited the Chignecto Historical Society, recently formed, to be present, and the formal proceedings of the day were under the auspices of the latter.

"After dinner, Judge Morse, as president of the Historical Society, in a neat speech spoke of the objects of the Chignecto Historical Society. It was their desire to find out who were the early settlers, and where they came from, and to collect all valuable information concerning the early history of this vicinity. He was pleased to see so many descendants of the original settlers of our country present, and see among them the most prosperous of our people. Mr. W. C. Milner, Secretary of the Society, then read an interesting paper on the expedition from New England to capture Fort Cumberland in 1776, under the command of Col. Eddy, and the influences that led to its defeat, notably the firm stand taken by the Yorkshire Royalists against the troops of the Continental Congress, and in favor of the Mother Land and the Old Flag. A good many facts connected with this episode in local history, which has been instrumental in shaping the destiny of the Province of New Brunswick, were for the first time made public. As it will be published in full in an early issue of the *Post*, together with other papers of the Chignecto Historical Society, it is unnecessary to reproduce it now.

"Judge Morse delivered an interesting address upon the Yorkshire settlers. The condition of our country in 1763 was one of constant strife between the French on the one side and the English on the other. But in 1763 the latter were victorious, the French driven back, and the country then thrown open for settlement by the English. In 1764 Governor Franklyn proposed to settle the very fertile land at the head of the Bay of Fundy with the proper class, and after some correspondence with Earl Hillsboro, Lord of the Plantations in England, he paid a personal visit to Yorkshire, where lived the thriftiest farmers in all England, induced in 1772-3-4 a large number of families to try their fortunes in the New World. In April and May the first arrivals landed on the bleak and rocky coast near Halifax, and surrounded as they were with every discomfort, it was no wonder that they felt discouraged. With their wives the men passed on to Windsor, where they first got a glimpse of the budding orchards left by the French settlers. Here a division was made in the party. The women and children were sent to the head of the Bay by a series of ferries, and the men pushed on to Annapolis, and later joined their families at Chignecto. To the pluck, loyalty, and industry of the Yorkshiremen Judge Morse paid many a tribute. To them do we owe our present connection with the Mother Country. When this country from north to south was rent by the rebellion, when the rivers ran blood, and when the prestige of English arms in Northern America seemed to totter, it was the Yorkshire immigrants who remained firm, and although compelled to suffer untold hardships and privations, yet they remained loyal to that old flag, whose folds he was pleased to see floating in the breeze to-day. The speaker gave fully in detail various particulars of the settlement, of the persons interested, and the location of several important landmarks. The York-shiremen have done three great acts: They made the country; they preserved the flag; and they, through the efforts of Preacher Black, founded in this country the principles of Methodism, which has made such steady progress, and which has been the prominent religion for over a century. He closed by asking all who had any historical relics in their possession to communicate with the officers of the society, and allow them to inspect such. Judge Morse was followed by Mr. A. B. Black, Amherst; J. L. Black, Sackville; W. C. Milner, and the host of the day, Mr. Howard Trueman, who spoke upon the valuable features of the Historical Society.

"Among those present were Sheriff McQueen, J. A. McQueen, M.P.P., W. J. Robinson (Moncton), Col. Wm. Blair, Hon. Hiram Black, J. L. Black, Wm. Prescott, Jas. Trueman, Esq. (St. John), W. F. George, Dr. A. D. Smith, Dr. H. S. Trueman, Rev. Mr. Crisp, Rev. Mr. Bliss, Couns. Copp and Trueman.

"The house at Prospect Farm is one of the oldest in the Province, having been completed on June 14th, 1799."

The following is an account of the one hundredth anniversary of the "Brick House," taken from the Moncton *Times* of July, 1899:

"On Friday, Prospect Farm, the residence of Howard Trueman, Esq., the old Trueman homestead at Point de Bute, was the scene of an anniversary that called together representatives of the various branches of the Trueman family that came to this country in 1775. The centenary of their settlement here was celebrated by a big picnic twenty-four years ago, and the present one was connected with the building of the old house one hundred years ago—a fine English house built of brick and overgrown with ivy and climbing rose. The site is one of the most commanding and beautiful in the country, and is justly a spot cherished by all the Truemans with pride and affection.

"The afternoon was charming, though threatening, and the numerous gathering, old and young, male and female, enjoyed themselves to the utmost.

"The oldest member of the family present was the venerable Martin Trueman, of Point de Bute, aged eight-four years, still hale and vigorous, and enjoying life as well as the youngest. The next oldest was Thompson Trueman, of Sackville, father of Mrs. (Senator) Wood, aged eighty-three, also a very vigorous man. Within a few weeks Mr. Joseph Trueman, also of the same generation, the father of Judge Trueman, of St. John, has passed to his rest. Mr. Henry Trueman, father of Mrs. James Colpitts, was prevented by the infirmities of age from being present. Amongst others of the same generation were Mrs. Eunice Moore, of Moncton, and Mrs. Amelia Black, of Truro, N.S. Others belonging to the older generation were James Trueman, of Hampton; Alder Trueman, of Sackville, and Benjamin Trueman of Point de Bute.

"A younger generation embraced Judge Trueman, of Albert; Pickard Trueman, James Amos Trueman, ex-Coun. Amos Trueman and George Trueman. There was a large representation present of those connected with Mr. Trueman by marriage or blood, as Squire Wm. Avard, Bristol; Collector Prescott, Bay Verte; Albert Carter, C. F. McCready, Sheriff McQueen, ex-collector James D. Dickson, George M. Black, I. F. Carter, James Main, Botsford; John Glendenning, Cumberland; Geo. W. Ripley, Mrs. J. M. Trueman, Thorndale, Pa; Gilbert Pugsley, Rupert Coates, Nappan; Hibbert Lawrence, Gilbert Lawrence, Burgess Fullerton, Southampton; Mrs. Sarah Patterson, Linden; Alex. Smith, Nappan; Dr. Chapman, James Colpitts, Point de Bute; J. L. Black, ex-M.P.P., Sackville; Mrs. Burke, Toronto; E. E. Baker, Fort Lawrence.

"Amongst the visitors were: R. Robertson, W. S. Blair, Experimental Farm, Nappan; Dr. W. F. Ganong, W. C. Milner, W. Fawcett, Charles George, W. F. George, John Roach, Thomas Roach, Nappan; Frank Beharrel, Lowell, Mass.; Dr. Allison, President Mt. Allison; Dr. Smith, Dr. Brecken, Prof. Andrews, Sackville; Rev. Mr. Batty, Amherst; Douglas Fullerton, Leonard Carter, J. H. Goodwin, Point de Bute; Hiram Copp, F. A. Dixon, Sackville; George Copp, James Fillmore, Bay Verte.

"A platform was erected under the shade of the vine-covered walls, and interesting speeches made. Dr. Chapman presided. In his introductory remarks he said he was pleased with his Yorkshire descent, and was very sorry that Mr. Batty, who was to tell sometime of Yorkshire at the present day, was not present. Mr. Howard Trueman, who was then called upon, told something of the settlement of the Truemans, the building of the house, the clock two hundred years old that was still keeping good time, the chair that came out from England with the family, and the bench there on the platform that came from the first Methodist church built in Canada, a stone church that stood by the Point de Bute Cemetery.

"Mr. J. L. Black spoke of his first visit to the old house. When not more than fourteen years old, he had been put on a horse and sent to the mill with a bag of wheat. On telling who he was he was sent to the house and fed with gingerbread and his pockets filled with cake. Mr. Black paid a high tribute to the sterling character of the men of the old days, but was of the opinion that the men of these days scarcely were their equals.

"Dr. Ganong, Mr. Milner and Mr. George not responding. Dr. Brecken was called upon. He claimed Yorkshire descent and supposed the stubbornness his wife complained of was due to the Yorkshire blood in him. He sometimes wondered, as Mr. Black had done, whether the race was not degenerating. He certainly could not stand as much exertion as his father could. The style of oratory was also very different from what it used to be. We have few of the finely finished speeches that characterized the old days.

"Dr. Allison said: 'All the speakers claimed some connection with the Truemans or Yorkshire, but he had not a drop of English blood in his veins, using English in its narrower sense. None, however, had a keener appreciation of the Yorkshire element than himself. Charles Allison, the founder of the Institutions, the one who had done more than any other to make the name of Allison to be remembered, chose for his partner in life a member of the Trueman family. Mankind was not degenerating. Wonderful things have been accomplished since this country was first settled. Divine providence has not constructed the railway and telegraph, but man. Dr. Brecken was just as good a man as his father, and a much greater orator than the men of those days. The men of the past suited the past, but a different type is required to-day.

"The chairman then announced that lunch would be served, and the other speakers would say a few words later in the afternoon.

"After lunch Judge Trueman, of Albert, took the platform. He said it gave him much pleasure to be at the picnic, not only to meet so many friends, but to see the old place where he was born and spent his youth. He knew every knoll and hollow of the old farm. He thought everyone who had the Trueman blood in him ought to feel on excellent terms with himself after hearing so many nice things said about the family.

"Prof. Andrews, who followed, agreed with Dr. Allison in thinking the race was not degenerating, and claimed if the people to-day would spend as much time out of doors as did their fathers, they would be even stronger. He gave some proofs that actually the race is improving physically. In the old times the weakest all died off, and only the tough old nuts remained. He told some remarkable stories of what he had undergone when a young man, that he claimed to be saving for his grandchildren. It gave him much pleasure to attend this celebration which would pass into history.

"Rev. Mr. Batty, of Amherst, was introduced by the chairman as a true bred, native-born Yorkshireman. Mr. Batty said, judging from the number around him, if all the Yorkshiremen had prospered as the Truemans there would be a new Yorkshire more prosperous than the old. He had not realized what kind of a picnic this was until he saw the lines of carriages driving through Amherst. On inquiring he found it was the gathering of the clans at Prospect. He considered these historic gatherings most important in the development of a country. He then gave a most interesting account of Yorkshire and Yorkshire Methodism. He had never seen a wooden house until he came to this country, and it stirred old memories to stand again under the shadow of a brick house that reminded him strongly of his grandfather's house in Yorkshire. If people here want to see Englishmen come to Canada they must do away with snake fences, sulphur matches, and bad roads. Agriculture is done for in England, and the fathers realize that their sons must come to Canada. No Westmoreland man would complain if he knew how well off he was.

"In closing he thanked all for their attention, Mr. Trueman for his invitation, and said he was going to write a full account of the gathering for the Yorkshire papers and send it at once.

"Votes of thanks were presented to Mr. and Mrs. Trueman, the host and hostess, and to Dr. Chapman, the chairman, after which all joined in the National Anthem."

The Chignecto *Post* had the following description of the gathering:

"The oldest house now being occupied in this part of the Province is in Point de Bute, about seven miles from Sackville. It was built in 1799, so that the structure is a hundred years old. In a granite slab over the front entrance is the following: "June 14, 1799." The main house is of brick and is a good solid looking structure yet. It has stood well the blasts of a hundred winters, and judging from its present appearance it will be able to stand many more.

"Some time ago the relatives and friends of Mr. Trueman urged him to celebrate the 100th birthday of his house. Circumstances prevented him from holding the celebration on June 14th, but on July 14th, last Friday, the event was celebrated in a manner that the two hundred people who were present will not soon forget.

"It was Mr. Trueman's intention that his guests should make a day of it, but unfortunately Friday forenoon was foggy and wet, and this no doubt prevented a large number from being present. However, the rain did not interfere with the plans of some of the friends, for early in the forenoon they began to arrive from a distance, and they continued to arrive, although the rain came down in torrents. But shortly after noon the cheerful face of Old Sol peered forth from behind a fog bank. The clouds were soon dissipated, nature dried her tears, and everybody was glad. A merrier throng it would have been hard to find than the one now gathered around the old brick house, everyone intent upon doing his or her best to celebrate the anniversary.

"There were people present from St. John, from Moncton, from Albert Co., from Bay Verte, from Amherst, from Nappan, from Sackville, and from all the surrounding country. There was the grandfather and grandmother, whose silvery hair and bent form contrasted strongly with sprightliness of the young toddlers who were very much in evidence. But a smile was on every face and nobody was made to feel that he was a stranger. From the top of the highest tree floated the Canadian ensign, while nearer the house the ancient folds of the Union Jack were spread to the breeze.

The Harmon Trueman House, built in 1806.

"The old house was thrown open to all, and many persons had the pleasure of seating themselves in the chair which was brought to this country by the first of the name who touched upon its shores. This article of furniture, together with a grandfather's clock, are the property of Mr. Trueman, and, needless to say, are very highly prized by him. They are remarkably well preserved, and the clock still keeps excellent time.

"On the grounds, quite near the house, a platform had been improvised, and during the afternoon short addresses were made by Howard Trueman, Jos. L. Black, Judge Trueman, of Albert Co., Rev. Mr. Batty, of Amherst, Prof. Andrews, Dr. Brecken, Dr. Allison and others.

"Tea was served on the grounds in true Bohemian style, but everybody enjoyed it. The evening passed very pleasantly with vocal, instrumental music, etc. It was a fitting celebration, and one which both old and young will no doubt often be pleased to look back upon. Mr. and Mrs. Trueman and the members of their family dispensed the kindest hospitality and did everything possible to make the event what it was, a grand success."

The names of the children and grandchildren of William Trueman and Elizabeth Keillor, with other records of the families:

HARMON TRUEMAN, born Sept. 27, 1778 } Married
CYNTHIA BEST, born Sept. 7, 1787 } Jan. 8, 1807.

### THEIR CHILDREN.

| NAME. | BORN. | M. | TO WHOM MARRIED. | CHILD. |
| --- | --- | --- | --- | --- |
| Stephen B. | Feb. 17, 1808 | 1836 | Eliza Wells | 7 |
| Amy E. | April 17, 1810 | 1837 | John W. McLeod | 1 |
| Sarah | Aug. 27, 1812 | 1835 | Rev. A. W. McLeod | 6 |
| Martin | Oct. 30, 1814 | 1843 | Bethia Purdy | 5 |
| Louisa C. | Aug. 30, 1817 | 1841 | Mariner Wood | 2 |
| Silas W. | May 27, 1820 | .... | Did not marry | .. |
| Eunice | Dec. 18, 1822 | 1872 | Thomas Moore | 0 |
| R. Alder | Aug. 22, 1825 | 1854 | Mary Jewett | 2 |
| N. Amelia | Sept. 28, 1828 | 1857 | Rufus Black | 5 |

WILLAM TRUEMAN, born Nov. 22, 1780 } Married
JANE RIPLEY, born April 25, 1788 } Jan. 22, 1806.

### THEIR CHILDREN.

| NAME. | BORN. | M. | TO WHOM MARRIED. | CHILD. |
| --- | --- | --- | --- | --- |
| William | Jan. 9, 1807 | 1831 | Esther Ripley | 9 |
| Mary Ann | Sept. 25, 1809 | 1834 | Francis Smith | 6 |

| | | | | |
|---|---|---|---|---|
| Jane D. | Dec. 20, 1811 | 1834 | Robert Fawcett | 7 |
| Alice | Jan. 2, 1814 | 1835 | Hugh Gallagher | 10 |
| Henry R. | Dec. 17, 1815 | 1844 | Jane Weldon | 2 |
| Joseph | Mar. 24, 1818 | 1843 | Janet S. Scott | 8 |
| Benjamin | Aug. 25, 1822 | 1848 | Elizabeth Weldon | 2 |
| Isaac | Jan. 18, 1825 | 1849 | Mary Black | 4 |
| Rebecca | July 12, 1827 | 1855 | Robert Scott | 6 |
| Sara Elizabeth | Sept. 26, 1829 | . . . . | John Charters | 4 |
| Christianna | Nov. 30, 1832 | 1856 | James Scott | 4 |

JOHN TRUEMAN, born Jan. 2, 1784 } Married
NANCY PALMER, born } 1806.

### THEIR CHILDREN.

| NAME. | BORN. | M. | TO WHOM MARRIED. | CHILD. |
|---|---|---|---|---|
| Catherine P. | April 30, 1807 | . . . . | John S. Coy | 4 |
| Gideon P. | Aug. 24, 1811 | . . . . | Mary Harrison | . . |
| Elizabeth L. | Sept. 8, 1813 | . . . . | Died young | . . |
| Thompson | Feb. 15, 1816 | . . . . | Rebecca Wood | 4 |
| Milcah | June 23, 1818 | . . . . | Chas. F. Alison | 1 |
| Marcus | May 10, 1821 | . . . . / . . . . | Rebecca Reynolds } 2 / Jane Evans } 2 } 4 |  |
| George A. | Sept. 26, 1823 | . . . . | Sarah Ann Black | 2 |
| Margaret C. | Mar. 2, 1826 | . . . . | Did not marry | . . |
| Annie J. | Mar. 30, 1829 | . . . . | Samuel Sharp | . . |
| Sarah B. | Sept. 6, 1832 | . . . . | Robt. A. Strong | 7 |

THOMAS TRUEMAN, born April 16, 1786 } Married
POLICENE CORE, born July 10, 1788 } July 11, 1805.

### THEIR CHILDREN.

| NAME. | BORN. | M. | TO WHOM MARRIED. | CHILD. |
|---|---|---|---|---|
| Elizabeth E. | Feb. 22, 1807 | 1825 | Thomas Carter | 4 |
| Able G. | Mar. 18, 1809 | . . . . | Died young | . . |
| William L. | Feb. 9, 1811 | . . . . / . . . . | Olivia Embree / Caroline Sharpe } 4 |  |
| Thomas F. | Feb. 9, 1811 | 1835 | Harriet Prince | 4 |
| Harmon Henry | July 21, 1813 | 1837 | Jane Chapman | 6 |

| | | | | |
|---|---|---|---|---|
| Lucy A. | Dec. 19, 1815 | 1835 | Joseph Carter | 4 |
| John Starr | Oct. 2, 1816 | .... | Died young | .. |
| Mary J. | Dec. 15, 1818 | 1841 | William Dixon | 0 |
| Rufus F. | Feb. 2, 1821 | 1846 / .... | { Eliza Trenholm / Francis Smith | 2 / 3 } 5 |
| Edward S. | Feb. 11, 1823 | 1847 | Sara L. Ann Bent | 5 |
| Frances B. | May 6, 1825 | 1849 | Samuel Sharp | 6 |
| Pamelia C. | May 31, 1827 | 1851 | William Smith | 4 |
| Charles E. | Apr. 24, 1829 | 1853 / .... | { Pamelia Smith / Susan Bowser | } 4 |

GILBERT LAWRENCE, born Oct.27, 1785      } Married
SARAH TRUEMEN, born Mar. 16, 1784        April 14, 1808.

### THEIR CHILDREN.

| NAME. | BORN. | M. | TO WHOM MARRIED. | CHILD. |
|---|---|---|---|---|
| David | Feb. 11, 1809 | 1836 | Mary Fullerton | 7 |
| William T. | May 9, 1811 | .... | Died young | .. |
| Sarah | Apr. 13, 1813 | 1833 | Daniel Pugsley | 6 |
| Mary F. | Oct. 1, 1815 | 1833 | Joseph Coates | 10 |
| Amos F. | Apr. 3, 1818 | 1841 | Annie Fullerton | 9 |
| Jane | July 14, 1820 | 1841 | James Fullerton | 3 |
| Charles W. | Nov. 19, 1822 | 1846 | Mary Fullerton | 1 |
| | | 1872 | Amelia Donkin | .. |
| Eunice M. | Feb. 27,1825 | 1847 | Jesse Fullerton | 7 |
| Thomas J. | Apr. 6, 1828 | .... | Did not marry | .. |
| Caroline A. | June 2, 1830 | 1851 | Douglas R. Pugsley | 2 |
| Cecelia R. | Apr. 4, 1833 | 1856 | David P. Fullerton | 6 |

AMOS TRUEMAN, born May 23, 1791      } Married
SUSANNA RIPLEY, born Feb. 20, 1799      October 2, 1817

### THEIR CHILDREN.

| NAME. | BORN. | M. | TO WHOM MARRIED. | CHILD. |
|---|---|---|---|---|
| Ann | July 2, 1818 | 1850 | Robert J. Mitchell | 5 |
| John | Oct. 2, 1819 | 1840 | Jane Finlay | 6 |
| Mary | Aug. 20, 1821 | .... | | .. |
| Henry | Sept. 10, 1824 | 1851 | Sophia Finlay | 7 |

| | | | | |
|---|---|---|---|---|
| Elizabeth | Dec. 24, 1826 | 1851 | Thomas Mitchell | 9 |
| Jane | Mar. 10, 1829 | .... | Did not marry | .. |
| Ruth | Sept. 9, 1831 | 1856 | Embree Wood | 8 |
| Rebecca | Apr. 21, 1834 | 1852 | William Mitchell | 4 |
| Susanna | Nov. 18, 1836 | 1863 | Joseph Doyle | 5 |
| Sarah | July 8, 1840 | 1865 | David Patterson | 6 |

ROBERT TRUEMAN, born July 15, 1794 } Married
EUNICE BENT, born Feb. 15, 1796 } January 8, 1817.

## THEIR CHILDREN.

| NAME. | BORN. | M. | To Whom Married. | CHILD. |
|---|---|---|---|---|
| James | Oct. 29, 1817 | 1844 | Jane Black | 2 |
| Seraphina A. | Apr. 28, 1819 | 1840 | J. W. McLeod | 6 |
| Calvin G. | Mar. 24, 1825 | .... | Did not marry | .. |

WILLIAM HUMPHREY, born } Married
MARY ANN TRUEMAN, born July 10, 1796 } Nov. 21, 1820

## THEIR CHILDREN.

| NAME. | BORN. | M. | To Whom Married. | CHILD. |
|---|---|---|---|---|
| William | Oct. 24, 1821 | 1863 | Hattie H. Sears | .. |
| John A. | Dec. 23, 1823 | 1855 | Sarah Harris | 4 |
| Elizabeth | May 19, 1825 | 1845 | E. R. Bishop | 5 |
| Stephen | Feb. 28, 1829 | 1851 | Lucy Logan | 6 |
| Harmon | July 12, 1831 { | 1859 | Salina Coates | 4 } 5 |
| | | 1878 | Emily Dixon | 1 } |
| Jane | Nov. 19, 1833 | 1854 | Joseph L. Black | 1 |
| Christopher | Apr. 15, 1837 | .... | ................ | .. |

GEORGE GLENDENNING, born May 14, 1799 } Married
BETTY TRUEMAN, born Aug. 11, 1798 } 1823

## THEIR CHILDREN.

| NAME. | BORN. | M. | To Whom Married. | CHILD. |
|---|---|---|---|---|
| Elizabeth S. | Jan. 28, 1825 | 1852 | Thomas Lowther | 8 |
| John | Sept.22, 1827 | 1850 | Elizabeth Black | 4 |
| Sarah Ann | Sept.27, 1829 | 1875 | David Lawrence | .. |
| William R. | Dec. 20, 1831 | .... | ................ | .. |

| Thompson | Oct. 26, 1834 | 1864 | Sarah J. Ripley | 2 |
| Mary | Aug. 28, 1837 | 1865 | J. Edward Smith | .. |

THOMPSON TRUEMAN, born 1801            ) Married
MARY FREEZE, born 1798                 ) 1823

### THEIR CHILDREN.

| NAME. | BORN. | M. | TO WHOM MARRIED. | CHILD. |
|---|---|---|---|---|
| Ruth A. | Jan 21, 1824 | .... | Did not marry | .. |
| Albert | Apr. 18, 1826 | .... | Did not marry | .. |
| Hiram | June 2, 1828 | 1854 | Tryphena Black | 6 |
| Eliza | Jan. 2, 1831 | 1855 | William Avard | 4 |
| Margaret | Nov. 11, 1835 | 1864 | George M. Black | 3 |
| Howard | Mar. 1, 1837 | 1863 | Agnes Johnstone | .. |
|  |  | 1867 | Mary J. Main | 5 |
| Mary A. | Dec. 26, 1843 | 1873 | William Prescott | 6 |

It will be seen by studying this record that out of the eight-seven members of the second generation born in this country, six elected to live in single blessedness. These were Silas, Harmon's third son; Thomas, a son of Sarah Lawrence; Margaret, a daughter of John; Jane, a daughter of Amos; and Ruth and Albert, Thompson's two eldest born.

Silas was a man of sterling principles, generous almost to a fault, and of more than ordinary intellectual force. He was the kind of man that would have delighted the practical mind of the Apostle James. Under all circumstances his aim was to make his practice accord with his profession. His death took place at his home in Point de Bute in 1860.

Thomas Lawrence was a general favorite, and had the reputation of being better to others than to himself. Children trusted him at once. He died at his home in Nappan, N.S., in 1867.

Margaret Trueman was one of the most charitable of women, always ready with a kind word or deed whenever opportunity offered. She finished life's journey in Mexico, in 1897.

Jane Trueman is still living.

Albert died in September, 1901, at his home, Prospect Farm. He was born in the brick house, and lived there his full life of seventy-five years and five months. He had many friends and no enemies.

Ruth lived her life of sixty-three years in the old home where she was born, and died in 1887. She was thoughtful and fond of reading, and did what she could to cultivate a taste for reading in those who came under her influence. Her religious convictions were decided, but not demonstrative. She delighted in conversation where literature and authors were the subjects. Macaulay was one of her favorite writers.

When Ruth's brothers and sisters were young, and books were not so common as now, she very often read aloud to her mother and the family. Macauley's Essays and History, Prescott's works, the "Literary Garland," and lighter works were read from time to time as circumstances or taste dictated. *Gleason's Pictorial,* the *Anglo-Saxon,* the *Scottish-American,* and *Harper's Magazine* were read with great interest. She was a subscriber to the *Century Magazine* at the time of her death. Some of Hannah More's sacred dramas were frequently read on a Sabbath evening. The writer remembers well how we younger children enjoyed the moment when David,

"From his well-directed sling, quick hurled,
With dexterous aim, a stone, which sank deep-lodged
In the capacious forehead of the foe."

And

"The mighty mass of man fell prone,
With its own weight, his shattered bulk was bruised.
Straight the youth drew from his sheath the giant's pond'rous sword,
And from the enormous trunk the gory head, furious in death,
he severed."

The language was rather beyond us, but we knew that David had killed the giant, and we did not bother about the big words. Or, when little Moses was left in the ark of bulrushes, exposed to all the dangers of the Nile swamp, how we almost trembled lest some evil should befall him before Pharaoh's daughter could rescue him, and rejoiced to think that Miriam did her part so well as to get her mother as a nurse for the little brother. Ruth seemed to enjoy reading these dramas over and over quite as much as we enjoyed listening to them. She grew fonder of reading as she grew older, and would talk of the characters in a book as if they were as real to her as her personal friends.

Ruth was deeply interested in the confederation of the Provinces when that question was before the people. After giving the matter a good deal of thought she decided in favor of the union. In early days, because of sympathy for a friend, she had conceived a prejudice against Dr. Tupper, who began his public life in Point de Bute, and with whom she was personally acquainted. The family at Prospect were supporters of Howe and the Liberal party in Nova Scotia at this time, but Howe had turned his back on Confederation, and Dr. Tupper was the leader of the Confederate party in that Province. Ruth was exceedingly anxious that the principle of union should triumph, and it was a grief to her that Dr. Tupper should triumph with it. But she lived long enough to forgive him and to appreciate the good work Sir Charles did for Canada.

The Free School question was another problem in which she was greatly interested, and as one of her favorite cousins was in the election of 1872, in which free non-sectarian schools were on trial in New Brunswick (at least, so thought the friends of this measure), she was anxious as to the outcome of the elections, and well pleased when they resulted well for free schools.

Of the twenty members of the second generation now living, the women out-number the men thirteen to seven. Five of the twenty are octogenarians, two—Martin Trueman, of Point de Bute, and Thompson Trueman, of Sackville—have reached the patriarchal age of eighty-seven years. The former in one particular is like the late Mr. Gladstone—he takes his recreation with the axe. He has prepared many cords of wood for the stove in the last few years.

The first Trueman family were not strong men, but they were persistent work-ers, and could accomplish more in a given time than men of much stronger build. The second generation were physically equal or superior to that of the first, which was rather a rare circumstance in this country. The gift of language—of talking easily and gracefully, either in private or public—was not one of their possessions. Not a man of the first generation could talk ten minutes on a public platform; and the second generation are in this particular not much of an improvement on their forbears. This, in part, no doubt, accounts for the fact that a family which turns out elders, class-leaders and circuit stewards in such numbers has not produced a minister of the Trueman name.

Agriculture was the work to which the family set their hand in the new coun-try. The children were taught that manual labor was honorable, and that agricul-ture was worthy of being prosecuted by the best of men. The seven sons and three sons-in-law were all successful farmers, and heredity no doubt had its influence.

# CHAPTER IX

## FAMILIES CONNECTED BY MARRIAGE
## WITH THE SECOND GENERATION OF TRUEMANS

### WELLS

WILLIAM WELLS, the first of the name in Point de Bute, was one of the Yorkshire band. He was a mason by trade, and built the Methodist Chapel at Thirsk before leaving Yorkshire. He married Margaret Dobson. The Dobsons lived in Sowerby, near Thirsk, and were among the first to accept the teachings of John Wesley. Mr. Wells did not come direct to Halifax, but landed at Boston, and, after staying there some months, came to Fort Cumberland. This was in 1772. He bought property in Upper Point de Bute, very near to that of his father-in-law, George Dobson. This property is still in the name of its original owner, a rare thing in this country, as very few families hold the same property for a century and a quarter.

Mrs. Wells was the mother of thirteen children, six of whom died in early life. The remaining seven married and settled in the country. They were married as follows:—George to Elizabeth Freeman, of Amherst; William to Catherine Allan, of Cape Tormentine; Mary to George Chappel, of Bay Verte; Elizabeth to Jonas Allan, of Cape Tormentine; Margaret to S. Freeze, of Amherst Point; Jane to Bill Chappell, of Bay Verte; and Joseph to Nellie Trenholm, of Point de Bute.

William Wells was an active member of the Methodist Church. He enjoyed a special gift in prayer, and not infrequently, in the absence of the minister, read the burial service over the dead.

I find this entry in the old journal: "June 3rd, 1811—Mrs. Jane Fawcett departed this life May 31st, very suddenly; was well about ten o'clock, and died before eleven o'clock; was buried Sunday afternoon by Wm. Wells, Esq."

The following letter, written a century ago by Mr. Wells, may have some interest for his descendants. The letter was addressed to William Trueman.

"DEAR BROTHER—Am sorry to hear of Mr. Bennet's indisposition, but am glad his case is hopeful. I trust the Lord has more work to do for him yet. Respecting myself should be glad to come to see my dear friends, but the journey appears to be too much for me to perform, for I was exceeding bad yesterday, and altho this day I feel a little freer from pain, yet my weakness is great. If

I should be better towards the latter part of the day maybe I may try to come, but I have hitherto felt worse at the latter part of the day. I pray God that our light afflictions may work out for us a far more and exceeding weight of glory.

"Yours affec.,
W. WELLS.

"Saturday morning,
"Nov. 13th, 1802."

The descendants of William Wells are widely scattered over New Brunswick and Nova Scotia, and a good number have emigrated to the United States. Charles H., Charles C., James, and Joseph D. Wells, great-grandsons, represent the name in Point de Bute and Jolicure. The late W. Woodbury Wells, M.P.P., and Mr. Justice Wells, of Moncton, also are members of this family, while Lieut.-Governor Snowball is a great-grandson of William Wells.

## BLACK.

William Black was born in Paisley, Scotland, in 1727. When a young man he removed to Huddersfield, England, and engaged in the linen and woollen drapery business. In 1774 he prospected Nova Scotia with a view to settlement, and purchased a large block of land near the present town of Amherst. The next year he brought his family, consisting of wife, four sons and a daughter, to Nova Scotia, and settled on his new farm.

William Black was twice married, and lived to the great age of ninety-three years. He spent the last years of his life in Dorchester, where he left a large family by his second wife. He was the father of William Black, who has been designated the "Father of Methodism" in the Lower Provinces.

The Blacks have proved good citizens, and have contributed their full share to the development of the country.

## PURDY

The Purdys were Loyalists from New York State. Three brothers came to this country—Henry, Gabriel, and Gilbert. Jacob, the fourth, remained in New York.

Henry Purdy settled in Fort Lawrence, Gabriel in Westchester, and Gilbert in Malagash. Mrs. Martin Trueman is a grand-daughter of Gilbert. The Purdys of Cumberland are all descendants of these brothers.

The family for the last century has always been able to count an M.D. among its members, and the civil service has seldom been without a Purdy on its roll-call.

## WOOD.

"The earliest record of the Wood family is the marriage of Thomas Wood and Ann Hunt, May, 1654, at Rowley, Mass. Their son John, born in 1656, married, in 1680, Isabel, daughter of Edward Hazen, presumably a forbear of the St. John Hazens. Issue of this union was a large family, of whom, Josiah, born April, 1708, was the twelfth child. He married Eleanor — — —, and their son, Josiah, born March, 1740, was married in 1767 to Ruth Thompson. Their son Josiah, born 1776, after coming to New Brunswick, married Sarah Ayre, daughter of Mariner and Amy Ayre. Their two children, Mariner and Ann, were the father and aunt of the present Josiah Wood.

"Mr. Wood has a number of interesting documents of ancient date, among them two grants of land from the King to Robert Thompson, the great-great-grandfather of Senator Wood. The earliest, dated 1759 (in the reign of George II), was for 750 acres, one and a half shares of the original grant of the township of Cornwallis. The later document attests that in 1763 Robert Thompson was granted 500 acres more, individually by George III.

"Mr. Thompson does not appear to have gone into possession, and some forty years later his widowed daughter, ambitious for the welfare of her fatherless family, set out from Lebanon, Conn., with her son Josiah to find this lost heritage.

"They appear to have come to Dorchester, N.B., by a schooner commanded by one 'Lige Ayre, so called. Why they should have gone first to Westmoreland's shire town, instead of direct to the Eldorado of their dreams is one of the unknowable things, but presumably the exigencies of travel in those days had something to do with it. Both passengers and mail matter went by dead reckoning, so to speak, and could seldom get direct conveyance to their destination.

"In the yellowed leaves of a century old diary, penned by the hand of Senator Wood's grandfather, and also from letters, we find quaint comments and an interesting insight into the lives of the early settlers.

"The journal was begun in October, 1800, when Josiah Wood was twenty-four years old. He and his mother, after visiting in Canard, appear to have made their home for the time being in Newport, N.S., where in the cloth mill of Alexander Lockhart Josiah found employment. The young man seems to have had all the business acumen and habits of industry that distinguish his posterity. When work in the mill was slack he taught school, beginning with four scholars. Evening amusements consisted of husking parties, etc., where Mr. Wood contributed to the festivities by flute playing and songs. His idea of a vacation was taking a load of cabbages to sell in Windsor, where his sole extravagance was buying a bandana handkerchief.

"Mrs. Wood filled in her time, though hardly profitably, by having smallpox. This dread disease did not seem to cause any dismay in those days. The neighbors came and went with kindly ministrations to the sick woman, and the son pursued his work in the mill, quite unconscious that according to modern science he was weaving the death-producing microbe into every yard of cloth.

"In February, 1801, Mrs. Wood and Josiah went to Halifax, where they put up the sign 'The Bunch of Grapes.' The diary speaks of their visiting 'Mr. Robie, Mr. Blowers, the Chief Justice and the governor,' with regard to their land, but to no purpose, their claim being considered invalid.

"In the fall of the same year they returned to Dorchester, where Josiah not long after married Miss Ayre. He died in his early thirties, leaving two young children, Mariner and Ann. The widow married Philip Palmer and afterwards went to live in Sackville, N.B. They had eight children, Martin, who settled in Hopewell Cape; Dr. Rufus Palmer, of Albert; Stephen Palmer, of Dorchester; Charles Jabez, and the Misses Palmer, of Sackville, and Judge Palmer, of St. John.

"Miss Ann Wood went to live with her grandmother at Fort Lawrence, while Mariner continued with his stepfather, commencing business in a small way on his own account at an early age. He purchased in course of time the property adjoining Mr. Palmer's, in Sackville, where he built a store and dwelling which is known as "The Farm," and continued his ever growing business at the same stand till his death, in 1875. In 1871 the firm assumed its present name of M. Wood & Sons.

"During his genealogical research Senator Wood has found relatives whom his branch of the family had lost sight of for a century. The Senator's grandfather had a brother, Charles Thompson Wood, born at Lebanon, Conn., October, 1779. He married Elizabeth Tracy, and pursued the trade of hatter in Norwich, Conn. He died in 1807, leaving two children, Charles Joseph and Rachel Tracey, both of whom married and in 1830 moved to Kinsman, Ohio.

"The children of this Charles J. Wood are living at Kinsman, and Senator Wood visited his long lost relatives this autumn. The pleasure was mutual, and while the Senator would tell of many years' patient seeking for his father's kindred, they related the story which had been told them by their father of his uncle, who had gone to the wilds of Canada and never been heard of more." —*Miss Cogswell in St. John Daily Sun.*

## McLEOD.

Alexander McLeod was born on board ship in Dublin harbor, the 11th December, 1773. His father belonged to the 42nd highlanders, a regiment then on its way to augment the British force in America. This regiment was on active service during the American Revolutionary war, and at its close was disbanded and grants of land in the Maritime Provinces distributed among its members. The greater number of these grants were on the Nashwaak River, in New Brunswick. Alexander McQueen, an officer in the same regiment, grandfather of Alexander McQueen, of Shediac, and great-grandfather of Sheriff McQueen, of Westmoreland, settled in Pictou County, N.S.

Mr. McLeod settled on the Nashwaak, and lived there the remainder of his life. Alexander, his son, went to Sheffield in 1796, and began a mercantile business. He married Elizabeth Barker, of that place. In 1806 he removed to the city of St. John, where for some years he conducted business on a scale large for the times, and was very successful. He was a Methodist local preacher, and in 1829 started a literary and religious journal, which enjoyed, like most of its successors in that city, but a brief existence. Mr. McLeod's family numbered six—Roderick, the youngest, died in infancy; Annie, the eldest, was a teacher and never married; Sarah married James Robertson; Margaret married Rev. Albert Desbrisay, who was for some years chaplain of the old Sackville Academy; Wesley was twice married, first in 1836, to Amy Trueman, who died, leaving one daughter; and again, in 1840, to Seraphina Trueman.

Wesley McLeod was a persistent reader, a good conversationalist, and a most interesting man to meet. He was a bank accountant, and the last forty years of his life were spent in the United States. His home was in Newark, N.J., where his widow and three daughters still live. Mr. McLeod never lost his love for the old flag for which his grandfather fought, and although so many years of his life were spent in the United States, where he always took a great interest in all public questions, he never became a naturalized citizen of the Republic. He lived to be eighty-five years of age. Robert Trueman McLeod, of Dunvegan, Point de Bute, is a son of Wesley McLeod.

Alexander first married Sarah Trueman, of Point de Bute, by whom he had five children. His second wife was Georgina Hultz, of Baltimore, U.S.

Robert, the youngest son of the first family, was in the Confederate Army in 1860, and lost an arm at Fort Sumter. He afterwards graduated with honors from Harvard and died in Europe while travelling for the benefit of his health.

Alexander McLeod was a Methodist preacher, and a Doctor of Divinity when that title was not so common as it is now. He was one of the editors of the *Provincial Wesleyan*. Like his brother Wesley, the last years of his life were spent in the United States, where both he and his wife were engaged in literary work.

The following extract is taken from a letter written by a member of the McLeod family in reply to one asking for information:

> "Your letter was received a couple of days ago and I would gladly send you all the information we have, but the most of it is so vague that it is quite unsatisfactory for your purpose. Of course we all know very positively that the McLeods sprang from the best and most honorable clan of old Scotland. We have improved some in manners, for we no longer drive our foes into caves, and smoke them to death. (We only wish we could.) We no longer brag that we were not beholden to Noah, but had boats of our own— that would relate us too nearly to Lillith— but still we are proud of our ancestors."

## AVARD.

Joseph Avard was born in the town of St. Austle, Cornwall, England, in 1761. At twelve years of age he was apprenticed to a clockmaker, with whom he remained eight years. He married Frances Ivey, in 1782. Mr. Avard was appointed a class-leader, and for seven years never failed to be present at the regular meeting of its members. He was intimately acquainted with Mr. Wesley, and attended his funeral, at which there was said to be thirty thousand people present. He also heard Charles Wesley preach his last sermon.

In 1789 Mr. Avard was one of nine charter members of the Strangers' Friend

Society, organized by Dr. Adam Clark. The object of the Society was the relief of distressed families in the town of Bristol where Mr. Avard lived. He was made a local preacher in 1790. For a short time he lived in London, and a daughter was buried in the City Road burying-ground. In 1806 Mr. Avard emigrated to Prince Edward Island, landing at Charlottetown on May 15th, where he remained until 1813. In the fall of that year he left Charlottetown, with the intention of going to Windsor, N.S., but on reaching Bay Verte he decided to stay the winter in New Brunswick. A part of the time was spent in Fort Lawrence, and in the spring he removed to Sackville, where he made his home until near the close of life. He died at his son's home, in Jolicure, in his eighty-seventh year.

Of the three children that came with Joseph Avard to America, Elizabeth married John Boyer, of Charlottetown; Adam Clark entered the ministry, and died in Fredericton, in 1821; Joseph was educated in Bristol, England, and soon after his arrival in America found his way to Chignecto and taught school several years in Point de Bute. In 1813 he married Margaret Wells, daughter of William Wells, of Point de Bute. They had a family of seven sons and four daughters, four of whom are still living-John, William and Charles, of Shemogue, N.B., and Mrs. McQueen, of Point de Bute. William married Eliza Trueman.

Joseph Avard, jun., was man of strong character, and when he set his will to do a piece of work he was generally successful. He settled first in Jolicure, where he conducted a farming and mercantile business. He subsequently bought a large tract of land in Shemogue, N.B., and for many years he was farmer, ship-builder and merchant in that locality, where he spent the last thirty years of his life.

In 1838, while on a business trip to River Philip, Mr. Avard was greatly shocked, as were the public in general, with the report that an entire family had been murdered in the vicinity, and that the man, Maurice Doyle, who was suspected of the crime, had escaped and was on his way to the United States, his aim being to get to St. John and take shipping there. As Doyle was known to be a desperate character, no one seemed willing "to run him down." As soon as Mr. Avard knew the state of affairs he at once volunteered to undertake the work. In the meantime Doyle had got a good start. At Amherst Head he hired a farmer, George Glendenning, to take him to the Four Corners, Sackville. Mrs. Glendenning was suspicious of the man, and advised her husband to have nothing to do with him, but Mr. Glendenning laughed at her fears. The dog, however, seemed to share his mistress's suspicions, and what was very unusual, determined to see his master through with the business. In spite of every effort the dog could not be turned back from following the chaise. Afterward, when Mr. Glendenning learned the character of the man, he believed the dog had saved his life, for in crossing the Sackville marsh, several miles from any house, Doyle asked him if the dog would protect him if he were attacked.

Mr. Avard always drove a good horse, and by changing horses and driving night and day he overtook and captured the fugitive at Sussex. At one place in the chase he prevented the man from getting on board the stage, but could not arrest him. When he finally apprehended the fugitive, he brought him back in his chaise and delivered him to the authorities in Amherst, where he subsequently paid the penalty of his crime on the scaffold. The documents following, as will be seen, refer to this piece of early history:

"Provincial Secretary's Office,

"Halifax, 10th July, 1838.

"Sir,—It appearing by the report of the Local Authorities at Amherst that the prompt arrest of the supposed perpetrator of the atrocious murders recently committed in the County of Cumberland is mainly attributable to your zealous exertions, I have it in command to request you to believe that His Excellency the Lieut.-Governor and H. M. Council highly appreciate the important services which, at much personal risk, you rendered in pursuing, for upwards of 100 miles, and apprehending the Prisoner; and it is my pleasing duty to request you to accept of the best thanks of His Excellency and the Council for your admirable conduct on that occasion. I have the honor to be

"Sir,
"Your most obedient
"Humble Servant,
"Rupert D. George.

"Joseph Avard, Esq., J.P.,
"Westmoreland."

Mr. Avard's reply.

"Westmoreland Co., Westmoreland,
"N.B., July 18th, 1838.

"Sir,—I have the honor to acknowledge the receipt of your note of the 10th instant conveying to me in a most gratifying manner the approbation of His Excellency the Lieutenant-Governor and Her Majesty's Council of my conduct in pursuing and apprehending Doyle, the supposed perpetrator of the murder in the County of Cumberland, and beg leave through you to acquaint His Excellency and Her Majesty's Council that were it possible for me to possess any stronger sense of my duty (as a magistrate) to Her Majesty and the Government than I formerly felt, I must do so from the very handsome manner in which they have been pleased to appreciate and acknowledge my services on that occasion.

"I have the honor to be
"Your obedient
"Humble Servant,
"Joseph Avard.

"The Honorable
"Rupert D. George,
"Provincial Secretary,
Halifax, N.S."

## DIXON.

Charles Dixon was one of the first of the Yorkshire settlers to arrive in Nova Scotia. He sailed from Liverpool on the 16th March, on board the *Duke of York*, and after a voyage of six weeks and four days arrived safely at the port of Halifax. Mr. Dixon says of himself: "I, Charles Dixon, was born March 8th, old style, in the year 1730, at Kirleavington, near Yarm, in the east riding of Yorkshire, in Old England. I was brought up to the bricklayer's trade with my father until I was about nineteen years of age, and followed that calling till the twenty-ninth year of my age. I then engaged in a paper manufactory at Hutton Rudby, and followed that business for the space of about twelve years with success. At the age of thirty-one I married Susanna Coates, by whom have had one son and four daughters." Three more children were added to Mr. Dixon's family, and in 1891 his descendants in America numbered 2,807, of whom 2,067 were living and 740 had died.

Charles Dixon settled in Sackville, N.B., and very soon became one of the leading men in that community. He was a zealous Methodist; his biographer says: "His house was a home for the early Methodist preachers, to whom he always gave a warm and hearty welcome." Mr. Dixon was one of the members who took an active part in the erection of the first Methodist church in Sackville, while he and his neighbor, William Cornforth, whose land adjoined, jointly set apart about four acres of land for a Methodist parsonage. One of the latest of his efforts at writing contained instructions to his executors to sell certain articles of his personal property to assist in furnishing the Methodist parsonage.

There are not many of the Dixon name now living in Sackville. The boys of the families have had a tendency to seek wider fields for the exercise of their energies. The late James Dixon, of Sackville, the historian of the family, was a man of strong character and more than ordinary ability.

William Coates Dixon married Mary J. Trueman in 1841, and resided in Sackville until the death of Mrs. Dixon, which took place in 1844. Subsequently he married Harriet E. Arnold and settled on a farm at Maidstone, Essex County, Ontario. James Dixon, in his "History of the Dixons," published in 1892, says of William Dixon: "He is still active and vigorous, capable of much physical exertion, and has an excellent memory, is a diligent reader, with a decided preference for poetical works, and employs some of his leisure hours in writing poetic effusions, a talent which only developed itself when its possessor had nearly reached his three score years and ten." We have not heard that Mr. Dixon has lost any of his vigor since the above was written, and understand he expects to round out the hundred.

## PRESCOTT.

The Prescotts were originally from Lancashire, and descended from Sir James Prescott, of Derby, in Lincolnshire. John and his wife, Mary, came from England to Boston in the year 1640. Jonathan Prescott, their great-grandson, was a surgeon and captain of engineers at the siege of Louisbourg, in 1745. After the fall of Louisbourg he retired from the army and settled in Nova Scotia. He did a mercantile business in Halifax, and owned property in Chester and Lunenburg, where he built mills. "The Indians twice burnt his house in Lunenburg County.' Mr. Prescott died in Chester, in 1806, and his widow in Halifax, in 1810. His son, Hon. Charles Ramage Prescott, was a prominent merchant of Halifax, but on account of failing health and to get rid of the fog moved to King's County, N.S. He lived for years at Town Plot, where his beautiful place, called "Acadia Villa," was situated. He was twice married. His first wife was Hannah Widden. The late Charles T. Prescott, of Bay Verte, was his youngest son by his second wife, Maria Hammill. Mr. Charles Prescott married Matilda E. Madden, April 30. William, Robert and Joseph, of Bay Verte, are sons of Charles T. Prescott. William married Mary Trueman, of Point de Bute.

## PRINCE.[5]

"MONCTON, March 9th, 1899.

"Dear Mr. Trueman:

"I have just received your card requesting information respecting my family. In answer I may say that my late father was a native of North Yarmouth, near the city of Portland, United States. He emigrated to this country in the year 1813, located in Moncton, and was engaged in mercantile pursuits until the time of his death in 1851, paying one hundred cents on the dollar. After taking the oath of allegiance he was appointed a magistrate, the duties of which he discharged with great fidelity until the time of his removal from earth.

"My father was a sincere Christian and a deacon in the Baptist Church, and died much lamented. His family consisted of twelve children, six sons and six daughters. May, the eldest, married a Mr. Gallagher and had several children, most of whom are dead. Emily, second daughter, married Mr. John Newcomb, father of the distinguished astronomer, Prof. Newcomb, of world-wide reputation. Joseph married Miss Harris. Harriet married Mr. Thos. Trueman. William has been an accountant in the railway offices of this city. John's wife was Miss Embree, of Amherst, and his second wife is Mrs. Cynthia, formerly Mrs. Mariner Wood. James resided in St. John; George and Henry, both dead. George never married; Henry resided in Truro at the time of his death and married to Miss Raine, daughter of Capt. Raine, a retired naval officer. Rebecca, Sarah and Ruth never married.

"As a family we were all as well educated as the circumstances would admit. My father's people in the United States were nearly all Congregationalists, and my great-grandfather Prince was a minister of that body. He was pastor of a church in Newburyport, and is buried in a vault under his pulpit. A few years

---

[5] Rev. John Prince was a respected minister of the Methodist Church. He joined the Church in Point de Bute and commenced his ministry there.

ago I visited that place, partly to see the church, which was built by my great-grandfather. When Sabbath morning came I went to the church; reached it just a little after the minister in charge had commenced the service. Seeing that I was a stranger, with somewhat of a clerical appearance, he came out of the pulpit to the pew where I was sitting, and said, among other things, 'We are going to have the Sacrament of the Lord's Supper to-day, and I would be glad to have you stay and assist,' which I did. At the close of the service I remarked to the minister that I was very much interested in being present, as I was informed that the remains of my ancestor were in the vault under the pulpit, and that I was his great-grandson. He seemed much surprised and announced the fact to the congregation, and further said that I would preach in the afternoon, which I did. He then directed the sexton to show me down into the vault. In this vault there were the remains of three ministers in their separate coffins. One was a coffin containing the remains of the immortal Whitfield. In the coffin just opposite was the remains of the Rev. Joseph Prince, and in another the remains of another former pastor of the church, Rev. Mr. Parsons. I certainly was very much impressed by my surroundings, for it was a scene the like of which I never hoped to look upon again. This vault, I was told, had been visited by thousands, who came to look upon George Whitfield's bones, for there was nothing but bones. Whitfield died a very short distance from the church, and the window of the house where he breathed his last was pointed out to me. I remember with what strange feelings I lad my hand on the shade of my ancestor. This man had twelve sons, and there was one thing about them the pastor said he knew, and that was 'that they were all Princes.'

"We can trace our ancestry back three hundred years, and the head of the family was Rev. John Prince, Rector of a parish in Berkshire, Eng. I have a photograph of the stone church where he ministered. His sons were Nonconformists, and John Prince, the first to come to this country, was persecuted and driven out of his country by the cruelty of Archbishop Laud..

"Yours very truly,
"JOHN PRINCE."

## CHAPMAN.

William Chapman was one of the Yorkshire emigrants that came to Nova Scotia in the spring of 1775. He brought with him his wife and family of eight children, four sons and four daughters. He purchased a large block of land near Point de Bute corner, with the marsh adjoining, and on this property at once settled.

William Chapman was one of the early Methodists, and it was in 1788, on an acre of land given by Mr. Chapman, and deeded to John Wesley, that the first

Methodist church was built in Point de Bute. Later, Joseph Chapman, Esq., a grandson of William, gave an additional piece of land, and the whole at the present time comprises the cemetery at Point de Bute.

The following letter from James Chapman, in Yorkshire, to William Trueman, at Prospect, will perhaps be interesting to some of the descendants. It was written in 1789:

"DEAR FRIENDS,—What shall I say to you? How shall I be thankful enough for that I have once more heard of my dear old friends in Nova Scotia. When John Trueman let me see your letter it caused tears of gratitude to flow from my eyes, to hear that you were all alive, but much more that I had reason to believe that you were on the road to Zion, with your faces thitherward. I am also thankful that I can tell you that I and my wife and ten children are yet alive, and I hope in good health, and I hope most of us are, though no earnestly pressing, yet we are feebly creeping towards the mark for the prize of our high calling of God in Christ Jesus. My son, Thomas, now lives at Hawnby, and follows shoemaking; he is not married, nor any of my sons. I have three daughters, Ann, Mary and Hannah. Ann succeeds her uncle and aunt, for they are both dead. Mary and her husband live on a little farm at Brompton, and Hannah at Helmsley. My son James is in the Excise at London. William and John are with me at home and George has learned the business of Cabinet maker. Prudence keeps a farmer's house in Cleaveland and Betty is at home and she is Taller than her mother. Thanks be to God both I and my wife enjoy a tolerable share of health and can both work and sleep tolerably well. _____ died about last Candlemas, which has made the society at Hawnby almost vacant for a class leader, but I go as often as I can and your friend, Benjamin Wedgewood, speaks to them when I am not there. Tho most of the old methodists at Hawnby are gone to Eternity, yet there is about thirty yet. James Hewgill is married and both him and his wife are joined in the society. There us preaching settled at Swainby and I believe a yearnest Society of aboyt Seventeen members. I often go there on Sundays to preach. There has just been a Confirence at Leeds and good old Mr. Wesley was there among them, very healthy and strong, though 86 years of age. At our Hawnby Love Feast I had Mr. Swinburn and his wife 2 nights at my house. They seem to be people who have religion truly at heart and both earnestly desired me to remember them Both to you in kind love and also to all their religious friends. I saw Nelly very lately at her house in North Allerton. She desires you all to pray for her, which she does for you all. My dear friends what Shall I say more to you, But only desire you to continue in the good ways of God, and never grow weary or faint in your minds, and then we hope to meet you in heaven. Pray give our kind loves to our old friends, your father and mother, and tell your Father when I see my Tooth drawers then I think of him, for he made them. My dear friends, farewell, our and our Family's kind love to you and all your Family, and also all the Chapman Familys, James and Ann Chapman. Mary Flintoff and Sara Bently are Both alive and remains at their old Habitations, But Mary never goes to the meetings. Their children are all alive, But Sarah Flintoff and she died at York about three or four years Since. James Flintoft is with his unkle George Cossins at London."

The Chapmans were very fond of military life, and in the old muster, days took an active interest in the general muster. As a consequence there was usually a colonel, a major, an adjutant or a captain in every neighborhood where the name was found.

A story is told of Captain Henry Chapman, on his way to general muster, meeting a man with a loaded team, whose hope was to get clear of mustering that day on the plea that he had not been long enough in the district. The captain ascertained the man's views on the matter, and then with an emphasis that indicated he was in earnest, he said, "If you are not on the muster field by one o'clock I will have you fined to the full extent of the law." One who witnessed this interview said it was laughable to see the frightened look on the man's face, and the rush he made to unhitch the team and get away to the muster field within the time stated. This same Captain Chapman was one of the kindest of men, but duty to Queen and country must not be neglected.

There was, too, a good deal of the sporting instinct in the family. A horse race or a fox hunt appealed to something in their nature that stirred the pulse like wine and furnished material for conversation on many a day afterward.

Like a good many of the first generation born in this country, the Chapmans were men of grand physique. The five sons of Colonel Henry Chapman, of Point de Bute, each measured six feet or over, and were finely proportioned. Two of the sons, Joseph and Stephen, were among the volunteers in the war of 1812, and they both lived to pass the four-score mark.

The children of the first Wm. Chapman were: William, who married a Miss Dixon, of Sackville, and settled in Fort Lawrence on a part of the old Eddy grant; and Thomas, who married Miss Kane, formerly a school teacher, from New England. They settled beside William. John married Sarah Black, of Amherst, and settled in Dorchester. Henry married Miss Seaman, of Wallace, and remained on the farm at Point de Bute. Mary married George Taylor, Memramcook. Jane married John Smith, of Fort Lawrence, and was the mother of nine strapping boys, all of whom proved good men for the country. Sally married Richard Black, of Amherst. They settled first at River Philip, but later came back to Amherst and lived on the farm his father first purchased in Cumberland. Nancy was twice married—first to Thomas Robinson, and after his death to James Roberts. Her home was in Amherst.

James Dixon, in his "History of the Dixons," says he thinks the descendants of William and Mary Chapman now number more than the descendants of any of the other Yorkshire families. Rev. Douglas Chapman, D.D., Rev. Eugene Chapman, Rev. Carritte Chapman, Rev. W. Y. Chapman, and Ephraim Chapman, barrister, are of this family.

The late Albert Chapman, of Boston, U.S., was very much interested in looking up family history, and spent a good deal of time in gathering information about the Chapman family. The following letters and extracts which were received by him some years before he died may add interest to this sketch:

> "13 Chipping House Road,
> "Sharrow, Sheffield, England,
> "Jan. 15th, 1881.

"Mr. Chapman,

"Sir,—You will no doubt be surprised to receive a letter from an unknown relative.

"We were much pleased to learn you had made enquiries about the Chapman family after so long a silence. We often heard father speak of uncle who left Hawnby Hall for America and could not get any letter answered. Most of the Chapman family have passed away since he left. We have the four grandchildren left belonging to Thomas Chapman, brother to your grandfather. The grandfather has been dead eighty years, and our father has been dead forty-five years.

"We should be glad to see you or any of the Chapman family if you could take a tour and see the place where your ancestors lived. The house and farm are still in the family and should be glad to accommodate you if you could come over, and we shall be glad to hear all the news about the family who lived and died in America.

"With best wishes to you and your,

> "I remain yours,
> "Mary Walton."

Extract from a letter from Thos. J. Wilkinson to A. Chapman, Boston:

> "York Union Bank,
> "Thirsk, Yorkshire.

"I have visited Hawnby a few times; it is most romantically situated about ten miles from Thirsk, rather difficult of access on account of the steep ascents which have to be climbed and precipitously descended before it can be reached.

"As I am acquainted with the clergyman who has been there many years, the Rev. O. A. Manners (connected with the Duke of Rutland's family) I wrote him and received the following letter:

"April 2nd, 1880.

"DEAR SIR,

"I have examined the register and found frequent mention of the name of Chapman of Hawnby Hall, viz., 'March 22, 1761 — John, son of William Chapman, Hawnby Hall, baptized. Feb. 3, 1763 — Thomas Chapman, of the Hall, died aged 75 years.'

"It would seem that the foregoing William Chapman was the son of Thomas Chapman and the man who landed in Halifax in 1775.

"About the latter date a family by the name of Barr came to reside at the Hall.

"James Cornforth of this place, who is in his 80th year, is related to this family. The said William Chapman being his great-uncle (maternal).

"The Hall is now, and has been for many years, a farm house.

"O. A. MANNERS."

The following names appear in the directory among the residents of Billsdale:

Joseph Chapman, Farmer
Robert Chapman, Farmer
Robert Chapman, Shoemaker
Robert Strickland Chapman, Farmer
Garbuth Chapman, Farmer, Dale Town.

## CARTER.

John Carter (the first) came from Yorkshire to Nova Scotia in 1774. His wife was Jane Thompson. They settled near Fort Cumberland, and had a family of three sons, Thomas, Christopher and John. Thomas married Miss Siddall and settled first at Westcock, Sackville Parish, but afterwards moved to Dorchester. Christopher married a Miss Roberts and settled at Westmoreland Point, near his father. John married Miss Anne Lowerison and remained on the homestead. The three brothers all had large families, the boys outnumbering the girls, which is the reason, no doubt, that the Carter name is more in evidence in the district than any other Yorkshire name.

John Carter's descendants still own the farm their great-grandfather first purchased in Nova Scotia. John Carter, sen., was drowned while fording the Missiquash River while on his way home from Amherst. His widow afterward became the second wife of William Chapman, of Point de Bute. Mr. Carter and his sons were honest men, and the name still stands well for fair dealing. Inspector Carter, of St. John, N.B.; Herbert Carter, M.D., of Port Elgin, N.B.; Titus Carter, barrister, of Fredericton, N.S., and Councillor Carter of Salisbury, N.B., are members of this family.

## TRENHOLM.

There were three Trenholm brothers in the Yorkshire contingent, Matthew, Edward, and John. Matthew settled at Windsor, Edward at River Francis, in the Upper Provinces, and John at Point de Bute on the Inverma Farm. This farm was probably confiscated to the Crown after Sheriff Allan left the country.

Just where Mr. Trenholm lived before he got possession of Inverma I have no information, but as Sheriff Allan had several tenants, it is quite probable that Mr. Trenholm was one of them. John Trenholm's wife was a Miss Coates. They had three sons—John, William, and Robert—and three daughters.

John married a Miss Foster and settled on a Brook farm at Point de Bute Corner and afterwards built a mill on the Brook. His grandson, Abijah, now owns this part of the property and turns out flour at the old stand. William married a Miss Ryan and owned a large farm in Point de Bute, on the north-west side of the ridge. Robert settled at Cape Tormentine in 1810, and the following table shows the names of his children and grandchildren:

| Children. | Grandchildren. | Children. | Grandchildren. |
|---|---|---|---|
| Stephen | 11 | Abner | 6 |
| John | 5 | Job | 10 |
| Hannah | 10 | Ruth | 12 |
| William | 10 | Thomas | 10 |
| Phoebe | 11 | Jane | 8 |
| Robert | 10 | Benjamin | 9 |
| | | Total | 112 |

Hiram and Abijah and their families are now the only descendants of the name living in Point de Bute.

The Trenholms were quiet, industrious men, very neat about their work, and made successful farmers.

## LOGAN.

Hugh Logan was one of the eleven hundred and seventy six settlers who, with their families, arrived at Chebucto (Halifax Harbor) on the 2nd of July, 1749. "This plan of sending out settlers to Nova Scotia was adopted by the British Government, and the lords of trade, by the King's command, advertised in March, 1749, offering to all officers and private men discharged from the army and navy, and to artificers necessary in building and husbandry, free passages, provisions for the voyage, and subsistence for a year after landing, arms, ammunition and utensils of industry, free grants of land in the Province, and a civil government with all the privileges enjoyed in the other English colonies."

Parliament voted £40,000 sterling for the expense of this undertaking. Colonel the Honorable Edward Cornwallis was gazetted Governor of Nova Scotia, May 9th, 1749, and sailed for the Province in the sloop-of-war *Sphinx*. On the 14th, of

June, just a month after leaving home, the *Sphinx* made the coast of Nova Scotia, but having no pilot on board, cruised off the land until the 21st June. On that day they entered Halifax Harbor.

Cornwallis writes, June 22nd: "The coasts are as rich as ever they have been represented to be. We caught fish every day since we came within forty leagues of the coast. The harbor itself is full of fish of all kinds. All the officers agree the harbor is the finest they have ever seen. The country is one continual wood, no clear spot is to be seen or heard of."

Mr. Logan entered into the spirit of the first builders of the new Province, and did his work to the best of his ability. His son, Hugh, came to Chignecto early in the history of the country and settled at Amherst Point. Hugh Logan was the founder of the family in Cumberland and became one of the solid men of the place. He is said to have been the owner of the first two-wheeled chaise in the district. Sheriff Logan, of Amherst, and Hance Logan, M.P. for Cumberland County, N.S., are descendants of Hugh Logan.

## ALLISON.

The Allisons came from the County of Londonderry, in Ireland, near the waters of Lough Foyle. Joseph Allison was born about 1720, and when he reached manhood's estate he rented a farm owned by a London Corporation, paying yearly rates, which were collected by an agent in Ireland. On the occasion of a visit from the agent to collect the rent he was invited by Mr. Allison to dine with them. The best the house afforded was given to him as an honored guest. On that day silver spoons were used. Turning to Mr. Allison the agent said, "I see that you can afford to have silver on your table. If you can afford this you can pay more rent; your next year's rent will be increased." "I will pay no more rent," said Mr. Allison, "I'll go to America first." The agent increased the rent the next year, and Mr. Allison sold his property and with his wife and six children, in 1769, left the home of his fathers and embarked from Londonderry for the New World. He intended to land at Philadelphia, having friends in Pennsylvania with whom he had corresponded and who had urged him to come to that State to settle. The passage was rough, and the vessel was wrecked on Sable Island, and Mr. Allison and his family were taken to Halifax, N.S.

Through the influence of the British Admiral Cochrane, then on the coast, Mr. Allison and the others that came with him were induced to settle in Nova Scotia. Mr. Allison purchased a farm in Horton, King's County, on the border of the historic Grand Pre, where he lived until his death, in 1794. His wife was Mrs. Alice Polk, of Londonderry. She survived him for several years, and gave the historic silver spoons to her youngest child, Nancy (Mrs. Leonard), who lived to be ninety years of age. They are now in the family of her great-grandson, the late Hon. Samuel Leonard Shannon, of Halifax.

Mr. Joseph Allison was a farmer. Many of his descendants have been prominent in the political, religious and commercial life of Nova Scotia in the last hundred years. A goodly number of these have stood by the fine old occupation of their ancestor.

Charles Allison (second), who married Milcah Trueman, was the founder of Mount Allison Educational Institution, at Sackville, N.B. His biographer says of him: "The name of no member of the Allison family is so widely known throughout Eastern British America as his," and "in him the noblest character was associated with the most unassuming demeanor." Charles and Joseph, brothers, were the first of the name to settle in Sackville. Dr. David Allison, President of Mount Allison University, and J. F. Allison, Postmaster, represent the name now in that place. The mother of the late Hon. William Crane, of Sackville, was Rebecca Allison, daughter of the first Joseph Allison.

## GALLAGHER.

The Gallaghers were a north of Ireland family. Hugh, who married Alice Trueman, was a most enterprising and capable man. He was a successful farmer and also a contractor. He built the last covered bridge over the Tantramar, a structure that was burned in the summer of 1901. He was also one of the contractors on the Eastern Extension Railway, from Moncton to the Nova Scotia border, and lost heavily by the Saxby tide. He was one of the pioneers in getting steamers to run to Sackville, before the railway was built, and part owner of the old steamer "*Princess Royal*," that ran on this route.

## SMITH.

Captain Smith came from Ireland to America at the beginning of the last century. He married a Miss Shipley. He was master of a schooner that ran between St. John and the ports at the head of the Bay. On his last trip the schooner took plaster at Nappan Bridge for St. John and was lost with all on board.

Francis Smith, son of Capt. Smith, married Mary Trueman, and had a large family. Mr. Smith was an honest and most industrious man. He left a large property at Nappan, N.S., to his sons, who inherited their father's virtues.

## COATES.

Thomas Coates emigrated from Yorkshire, England, to Nova Scotia in the year, 1774, and settled at Nappan, Cumberland County. His son, Robert, by his second wife, married Jane Ripley, and inherited the homestead. This property is now owned by his grandson, Rupert Coates. Joseph Coates, a son of Robert, married Mary Lawrence. They had a family of ten children.

Mr. Coates was a successful farmer and amassed a large property. His sons, Thompson and Rupert, are at the present time prominent men and leading farmers of Nappan, N.S. Another branch of the Coates' family removed to King's County, N.B., and planted the name there.

## FULLERTON.

James Fullerton was from the Highlands of Scotland. He came to Nova Scotia in 1790, and settled at Halfway River, Cumberland County. His wife was a Miss McIntosh. The eldest son, Alexander, was born before they left Scotland; and one son and three daughters were born in this country. Alexander had a family of three sons and five daughters. James married Jane Lawrence, and Jesse married Eunice Lawrence. The eldest daughter, Anna, married Amos Lawrence, and the youngest, Lavina, married Douglas Pugsley, of Nappan, whose first wife was Caroline Lawrence. James Fullerton (second) took an active interest in politics, and was a prominent man in the county for many years. He was one of the men that supplied the Halifax market with Cumberland beef. Although a stout man in late years, he was very active on his feet, and few men could out-walk him, even after he was seventy years old.

## EMBREE.

Samuel Embree was a Loyalist from White Haven, New York. He commanded the Light Horse Dragoons during the Revolutionary War, and at its close his landed estate was confiscated. He then left the country and settled in Amherst, N.S. The British Government did not forget his services for the lost cause, and he drew a pension to the end of his life.

Cyrus Black says, in his "History of the Blacks," that Mrs. Embree once distinguished herself on a trip from Eastport to the Isthmus. The captain was incapable of managing the boat through drink, and there was no man to take his place. Mrs. Embree took the helm and brought the schooner safe to Aulac."

Thomas and Israel, Mr. Embree's sons, remained on the homestead at Amherst. Elisha, a third son, settled at Amherst Head, now called Warren. A daughter married Luther Lusby. A grand-daughter of Israel married William L. Trueman.

## RIPLEY.

Six brothers came to America from Yorkshire. Henry, John and William Ripley came in 1774; Joseph, Robert, and Thomas, later. Henry settled in Nappan, and his wife was Mary Fawcett, daughter of John Fawcett, of Lower Sackville, N.B. Henry and Mary Ripley had a family of sixteen children. Henry Ripley occupied a rented farm the first years in this country, but later purchased a farm from the DeBarres estate, 600 acres of marsh and upland, for £600, and became a very prosperous farmer. The name is pretty well scattered, but there are Ripleys still in Nappan who, like their ancestors, are men of integrity.

## PUGSLEY.

The Pugsleys were Loyalists. David Pugsley came from White Plains, New York, to Nova Scotia, when a young man, and settled in Amherst. The one hundred acres of land given him by the Government was at Wallace. He was twice married. His first wife, by whom he had one son, was a Miss Horton. His second wife was a Miss Ripley, and had twelve children, seven daughters and five sons.

Mrs. Pugsley had a brother John, who was a half-pay officer in the British army. This brother lived a short time at Fort Lawrence, and had one son, named

Daniel. John Pugsley and his wife left this son with friends in Petitcodiac, and returned either to the States or to Great Britain. They were not heard from afterward. The Pugsleys of King's County and St. John are descendants of this Daniel. Those in Cumberland are descended from David. The Pugsleys are good citizens, and generally have the means and the disposition to help a neighbor in need.

## FINLAY—MITCHELL—PATTERSON—DOYLE.

The Finlays came from the north of Ireland about the year 1820. Jane Finlay, who married John Trueman, was born on the banks of Newfoundland, on the voyage out, and only just escaped being called Nancy, after the ship. David and Margaret Mitchell came from the neighborhood of Londonderry, in Ireland to Nova Scotia, in 1829. David Patterson came from Maghera, Culnady County Antrim, Ireland, in June, 1839. These families all settled in Cumberland County, bordering on the Straits of Northumberland. The Doyles emigrated to Nova Scotia, about 1790, and settled at Five Islands, Parrsboro.

It is said David Patterson studied for the church, and perhaps that, in part, accounts for the fact that four of his children are, or have been, teachers. A daughter has just offered and been accepted for the foreign missions. Mrs. Patterson writes: "Daisy has offered herself as a medical missionary and been accepted. She will leave for China next September, via San Francisco. It is something I can hardly talk about, yet I would rather she would go there than marry the richest man in the United States, for it is a grand thing to work for the Lord Jesus. I remember," she goes on to say, "of being told that grandmother Trueman had faith to believe God would save all her children and grandchildren down to the fourth generation, and don't you think we are reaping the fruit of grandmother's faith and prayers to the present day?"

Two sons of Thomas Mitchell are in the Presbyterian ministry.

Of this Scotch-Irish stock Hon. Charles Bell says: "The Scotch-Irish were people of Scottish lineage who dwelt upon Irish soil. They stuck together and kept aloof from the native Celtic race." Macaulay says: "They sprang from different stocks. They spoke different languages. They had different national characteristics as strongly opposed as any two national characters in Europe. Between two such populations there could be little sympathy, and centuries of calamities and wrongs had generated a strong antipathy. The Scotch planted upon Irish soil were Scotch still, and the Irish were Irish still." One of their own writers says: "If we be not the very peculiar people, we Scotch-Irish are a most peculiar people, who have ever left our own broad distinct mark wherever we have come, and have it in us still to do the same, even our critics being the judges. These racial marks are birth-marks, and birth-marks are indelible. They are principles. The principles are the same everywhere, and these principles are of four classes: religious, moral, intellectual and political."

I have been led to make these quotations referring to the Scotch-Irish because I have found so many of them among the early settlers of this country, and wherever they are found they have proved true to their lineage.

Others embraced in this emigration are: Clark, Moffat, Logan, Dickey, McElmon, McClennen, Allison, and Dickson or Dixon.

## FAWCETT.

Three brothers name Fawcett—William, John and Robert—came to Nova Scotia from Hovingham, Yorkshire, in the spring of 1774. William, with his and three children, settled in Upper Sackville, on the farm now owned by Charles George. John settled in Lower Sackville, near present Mount Allison Academy, and built a mill on the brook that runs through the farm. The Fawcett foundry stands on what was the bed of the old mill-pond. Robert was a sea captain. He removed his family to the United States and was afterwards lost at sea. One of his sons lost his life in the same way.

William's children were: John, William and Polly. John married Mrs. Eleanor Colpitts, nee Eleanor Forster, of Amherst, and had four children, George, Ann, William and Eleanor.

William (second) married Sarah Holmes. Their children were Rufus and Betsy.

Polly married John Dobson, who afterwards moved to Sussex. The Dobsons of Sussex and Upper Dorchester belong to this family.

John Fawcett (first), Lower Sackville, had four children—two sons, Robert and John, and two daughters, Mary and Nancy. Of these, Robert married — —-Seaman; John married Jane Black; Mary married Henry Ripley, and Nancy married John Ogden. Robert, a son of the second Robert, married Jane Trueman, daughter of William Trueman.

In 1817 (March 22nd) Thomas Fawcett, of Stockton Forest, Yorkshire, sailed from Hull on the ship *Valiant*, bound for Charlottetown, P. E. Island. The voyage lasted seventy-three days. About the middle of the voyage the *Valiant* came across a Scotch brig in a sinking condition and took on board her sixty passengers and crew. There were one hundred and ninety-three immigrants on the ship when she arrived at her destination.

Thomas Fawcett settled first at Cove Head, P.E.I. He afterward moved to Sackville, and finally located at Salisbury. He had three sons, one now living in Carleton County, N.B., one in Salisbury, and John is one of the solid men to Tidnish.

Other passengers on the *Valiant* were: John Milner, settled in Sackville; John Towse, settled in Dorchester; Robert Morrison, settled in Sussex; Robert Mitten and family, settled in Coverdale.

## EVANS.

Isaac Evans came to this country, probably from the United States, shortly after the close of the Revolutionary war. The family was originally from Wales. He was married to Miss Lydia Jenks, and settled within a few rods of the old Botsford place at Westcock. They had seven children, all born in this country—James, Isaac, William, Lydia, Mary, Ann and Beriah. James married Miss Barnes, and Mr. Isaac N. Evans, the only man of the name now living in the parish, is a son of theirs.

His name and his brother William's are to be found in the list of students attending Mount Allison Academy in 1843. Isaac drowned off Grindstone Island when twenty-four years old, in 1819. William married a Miss Estabrooks, and they had ten children—James Isaac, who died recently at Shediac, where his family still live; Evander Valentine, who lived in Sackville and was well known as Captain Evans; Jane, who married Marcus Trueman, and now lives in California; William Murray Stuart, who at one time had charge of the Westmoreland Bank in Moncton; George Edwin, a mechanic, who moved early in life to the United States; Henry, who served on the side of the North in the War of Secession; Charles, who married a daughter of the late John Fawcett, but died young. Lydia married Lewis Jenks; Mary never married, but lived to be old, and was known by her friends as "Aunt Polly"; Ann married John Boultonhouse, and Beriah married John Stuart. Isaac Evans, the original settler, was drowned off Partridge Island, St. John, June, 1798, aged thirty-four. Lydia, his wife, died November 11th, 1842, in her seventy-fourth year.

## WOOD.

William Wood was from Buriston, near Bedale, in the West Riding of Yorkshire. His wife was Elizabeth Clarkson. They emigrated to America with the first Yorkshire contingent (1772-3). Shortly after coming to this country Mrs. Wood died, leaving three children—a son and two daughters. The son was born on St. Valentine's Day, and was named Valentine. Mr. Wood's second wife was the widow of an officer who had served at Fort Cumberland. Mr. Wood was at the "Fort" when the Eddy rebels attacked that place, and distinguished himself by his bravery. He was drowned in the Bay of Fundy.

Valentine Wood married and settled in Point de Bute. His family consisted of eleven children: William, who died in boyhood; Edward, Rufus, Joshua, Cyrus, Thomas, Albert, Mary Ann, Cynthia, Amelia, and the youngest, Rebecca (Mrs. Thompson Trueman, of Sackville, N.B.)

Edward was named for an uncle in England. He made his home in Bay Verte, N.B., and became a most useful and acceptable Methodist local preacher. Two of the Wood family were teachers. Thomas W. was a prominent and successful educationalist. The Wood family were more than ordinarily gifted intellectually. Albert, the youngest son, became celebrated as a skilful and successful sea captain. He published a book, entitled "Great Circle Sailing," that quite changed the methods, in some particulars, from which ships had been navigated previously. Captain Wood finally settled in California, where he now lives, and is an enthusiastic temperance worker and writer. Joshua was musically inclined, and taught the old fashioned singing school. He possessed characteristics that made him quite a hero with many of his friends.

Most of the descendants of William Wood bearing the name have removed from the country.

## HARRIS.

The Harris name is one of the oldest in Canada. Arthur Harris came from Plymouth, England, to Bridgewater, New England, in 1650. He removed from there to Danby, and from Danby to Boston in 1696. His son, Samuel, was with Captain Ben Church's expedition to Acadia in 1704, and shortly after Acadia came into possession of the English he settled in Annapolis. Michael Spurr Harris, a grandson of Samuel Harris, was born at Annapolis Royal in 1804. His wife, Sarah Ann Troop, was born in Aylesford in 1806. Michael Harris started in business in St. John in 1826; in 1837 he removed his family to Moncton and opened a general store and carriage building establishment, and soon after added shipbuilding to the business. After his death the business was very successfully conducted for many years by his two sons, the late John Harris and Christopher Harris.

This firm was always abreast of the times, and the city of Moncton owes much to its enterprise and farsightedness. The late Mrs. John A. Humphrey was a daughter of Michel Spurr Harris.

## MAIN.

The Mains are Scotch. The family tree goes back to the beginning of the fifteenth century, one branch including the present Lord Rosebery and Sir William Alexander, who are one time owned Nova Scotia and gave the Province its name. David Main with two of his sons, John and James, emigrated from Dumfries. Scotland, to Richibucto, New Brunswick, in the spring of 1821, and settled at Galloway, on the farm now owned by Robert Main, a grandson of David, and son of James. James married Jane Murray, of Shemogue. James Main, of Botsford, is also a son of theirs. John married Jean Johnstone, and lived in Kingston, now called Rexton. Mary Jean Main, wife of Howard Trueman, is his daughter. The late David Main, of St. Stephen, was a son of John Main.

## SHARP.

Four brothers named Sharp came to the Isthmus from Cornwallis, N.S., about the year 1812. Matthew settled in Nappan, William in Maccan, Allan in Amherst, and John in Sackville. Samuel Sharp, who married Fanny Trueman, was a son of William Sharp.

## WELDON.

Two of William Trueman's sons married into the Weldon family. I am not able to give any more information about the Weldons than is found in the "History of the Blacks," which is as follows: "A Mr. Weldon left London for Halifax in 1760. The vessel in which he sailed was wrecked on the coast of Portugal. Returning to London, in 1761, he found that his wife and family had sailed for Halifax, where he joined them in the fall of the same year." Mr. Weldon settled first in Hillsboro and later removed to Dorchester, where the name has remained ever since. Dr. Weldon, Dean of the Halifax Law School, belongs to this family.

## SCOTT.

Adam Scott was from Langholm, Dumfriesshire, Scotland. He emigrated to New Brunswick with his wife and family in 1834, landing first at Quebec. He settled in Shemogue, Westmoreland County. His wife's name was Janet Amos. He had eight children. Two of the sons and the eldest daughter, Janet, married into William Trueman's family. The daughter, Mrs. Joseph Trueman, is still living, bright and cheerful, in the 84th year of her age. Mr. Scott was one of the most prosperous farmers in the district in which he settled, and lived to be ninety-nine years of age.

## BENT.

This name is believed to have come from bent grass, "a stiff, wiry growth, little known in America." John Bent, the first of the name in America, was born in Penton-Grafton, England, in November, 1596. He came to America in his forty-second year, and settled in Sudbury, Mass. The Bents came to Nova Scotia around 1760. The names of Jesse and John Bent are found on the list of grantees for the township of Cumberland in 1763, to which reference has previously been made. Sarah A. Bent, daughter of Martin Bent, married Edward Trueman.

## JEWETT—COY.

Mary Jewett, who married Alder Trueman, of Sackville, and Asa Coy, who married Catherine Trueman, of Point de Bute, were of the New England emigration that settled on the St. John River in 1762-3.

## HARRISON.

John Harrison, of Rillington, Yorkshire, England, and his wife, Sarah Lovell, of the same place with their family arrived in Cumberland County, Nova Scotia, in the spring of 1774, and settled on the Maccan River. They had family as follows: Luke, born August 25th, 1754, married Tryphena Bent, November 22nd, 1789; John, married twice, first wife Dinah Lumley, of Yorkshire, England, and second Charlotte Mills, of the State of New York; Thomas born March 28th, 1762, married Mary Henry; William, born March 25th, 1770, married Jane Coates; Mary, married Matthew Lodge; Sarah, married James Brown; Nancy, married John Lumley; Hannah, married John Lambert; Elizabeth, married Henry Furlong.

Luke Harrison (son of John) and his wife Tryphena Bent, had family as follows: Jane, married William Bostock; Margaret; George, married Sarah Hodson; Hannah married George Boss; Amy, married Thos. Dodsworth; Eunice, married Amos Boss; Elizabeth, married William Smith; Joseph; Jesse, married Elizabeth Hoeg.

John Harrison (son of John), whose first wife was Dinah Lumley, and second Charlotte Mills, had family as follows: Sarah, John, Maria, Lovell, Mary, Charlotte, Rebecca; William, married Elizabeth Brown; James.

Thomas Harrison (son of John) and his wife Mary Henry, had family as follows: Luke, married Hannah Lodge; Sarah, married Martin Hoeg; Clementina, married Joseph Moore; Harriet, married William Coates; Thomas, married Clementina Stockton; Tillott, married Eunice Lockwood; Mary, married Gideon Trueman; Ruth, married Hugh Fullerton; Henry, first wife Phoebe Chipman, and second A. M. Randall.

William Harrison (son of John) and his wife, Jane Coates, had family as follows: Sarah, married Robert Oldfield; Thomas, married Elizabeth Shipley; Edward; William, married Mary Tait; John, married Jerusha Lewis; Ann, married David Keiver; Joseph, married Jane Ripley; James, married Mary Lewis; Robert, married Hannah Wood; Jane, married Nathan Hoeg; Luke; Brown, married Mary Ann Coates; Hannah, married David Long.

Luke Harrison (son of Thomas and Mary), was born August 10th, 1787, and died November 12th, 1865. He and his wife, Hannah Lodge, moved from Maccan River, N.S., to Dutch Valley, near Sussex, N.B., and had family as follows: William Henry, married three times, first wife was Sarah Slocomb, second Rebecca Slocomb, and third Lavina M. Knight; Charles Clement; Mary Ann, married J. Nelson Coates, of Smith's Creek, King's County, N.B.; Thomas Albert, married Isabel Stevenson, of St. Andrew's, N.B.; Joseph Lodge, married Charlotte Snider, of Dutch Valley, Sussex, N.B.

William Henry Harrison (son of Luke Harrison and Hannah Lodge), was born July 20th, 1813, at Sussex, N.B., and died May 2nd, 1901, at Sackville, N.B. He had no family by his first and second wives. He and his third wife, Lavina M. Knight, daughter of Rev. Richard Knight, D.D., of Devonshire, England, had family as follows: Richard Knight, married to Anne Graham, of Sussex, N.B., living at Colorado Springs, Colorado, U.S.A.; Hannah Lovell, dead; William Henry, of Sackville, N.B.; Charles Allison, dead; F. A. Lovell, of St. John, N.B.; Albert Thornton, of New York City; Mary Louisa, married to T. Dwight Pickard, of Sackville, N.B., living at Fairview, B.C.; Frank Allison, of Sackville, N.B., married to Flora Anderson.

John Harrison, of Rillington, Yorkshire, England, who settled at Maccan River, N.S., Canada, in 1774, was a relative of John Harrison, born at Foulby, in the Parish of Wragley, near Pontrefact, Yorkshire, May, 1693. John Harrison, of Foulby, was the inventor of the chronometer, for which he received from the British Government the sum of £20,000. He died at his home in Red Lion Square, London, in 1776. The chronometer accepted by the Government from John Harrison was seen in July, 1901, at Guildhall, London.

The following letters were written by members of the Harrison family to friends in England.

William H. Harrison, a descendant of John Harrison, visited Yorkshire about the year 1854, and received the letters from friends there, bringing them back to Nova Scotia, where they were written so many years before. They are interesting as giving the experience of the emigrant in the new country. The first was written by Luke, a young man twenty years old, who had come to Nova Scotia with his father and had been in the country but three months. The second was written by John Harrison, a brother of Luke's, in 1803, after they had tested the country.

EXTRACTS FROM OLD LETTERS OF THE HARRISON FAMILY.

"To Mr. WILLIAM HARRISON,
"Rillington, Yorkshire,
"England.

"June 30th, 1774.

"DEAR COUSIN, — "Hoping these lines will find you in good health, as we are at present, bless God for it. We have all gotten safe to Nova Scotia, but do not like it at all, and a great many besides us, and are coming back to England again, all that can get back. We do not like the country, not never shall. The mosquitos are a terrible plague in this country. You may think that mosquitos cannot hurt, but if you do you are mistaken, for they will swell you legs and hands so that some persons are both blind and lame for some days. They grow worse every year and they bite the English the worst. We have taken a farm of one Mr. Barron, for one year, or longer if we like. The rent is £20 a year. We have 10 cows, 4 oxen, 20 sheep, one sow, and one breeding mare. He will take the rent in butter or cheese, or cattle. The country is very poor, and there is very little money about Cumberland. The money is not like our English money. An English guinea is £1 3s. 4d. In Nova Scotia money a dollar is equal to 5 shillings, and a pistereen is a shilling. In haying time men have 3 shillings a day for mowing. The mosquitos will bite them very often so that they will throw down their scythes and run home, almost bitten to death, and there is a black fly worse than all the rest. One is tormented all the summer with mosquitos, and almost frozen to death in the winter. Last winter they had what was reckoned to be a fine winter, and the frost was not out of the ground on the 20th day of June, which I will affirm for truth. I shall let you know the affairs of the country another year, if God spare life and health. Dear cousin, remember me to my uncle and aunt and to all that ask after me.

"From your well wisher,
"LUKE HARRISON.

"Direct your letters to John Harrison or Luke Harrison, at the River a Bare, nigh Fort Cumberland, Nova Scotia."

"To Mr. JOHN HARRISON,
"Rillington, near Motton,
"Yorkshire, England.

"Maccan River, N.S.,
"June 24th, 1810.

"DEAR COUSIN, —

"Long ago I have had it in agitation of writing to you and now an opportunity is just at hand, which I gladly now embrace, hoping these lines will find you and your family all in good health, as me and my family are the same, thanks be to him that ruleth over all. I am now going to give you a little sketch of our country, of Bonny Nova Scotia, and the advantages and disadvantages. I settled here on this river about 23 years ago, upon lands that had never been cultivated, all a wilderness. We cut down the wood of the land and burnt it off, and sowed it with wheat and rye, so that we have made out a very good living. Here we make our own sugar, our own soap and candles, and likewise our own clothing. We spin and weave our own linen and wool, and make the biggest part of it into garments within our own family. This, I suppose, you will think strange, but it is merely for want of settlers and more mechanics of different branches. There were twenty-five petitioned to the Government for new lands when I settled here, and we all drew 500 acres of land each. I bought 500 acres joining mine, which cost me about eighteen pounds, and my part of the grant cost eight pounds. I have lived on it ever since and make out a very good living. We milk ten cows, keep one yoke of oxen, three horses, betwixt twenty and thirty sheep. I do not doubt but that in the run of ten years more I shall be able to milk twenty cows. We generally kill every fall six or eight hogs. We use betwixt four hundred and five hundred pounds of sugar every year for tea and other necessaries. The disadvantage we have here is in the winters being so long. There is six months to fodder our cattle, and what is worse than all the rest, the snow falling so deep, sometimes four feet. The last three or four winters have been very moderate, which we think is owing to the country and woods being cleared more away. We have very much trouble with bears, as they destroy our sheep and cattle so much.

"JOHN HARRISON.

"N.B.—I have two sons, up young men. Pray send them each a good, industrious wife. Pray send out a ship-load of young women, for there is a great call for them that can card and spin. The wages are from five to six shillings a week."

# CHAPTER X

## THE FIRST SETTLERS OF CUMBERLAND

IN the early part of the last century several emigrants from the Old Country found their way to Prospect Farm, with whom family friendships were formed and remained unbroken for many years. The Davis family is one of these.

Daniel Davis came from a small town near Bristol, England. He was a weaver by trade, but owing to the introduction of the power loom in Great Britain, which ruined the hand-loom industry, Mr. Davis came to America in the hope of finding some other means of gaining a livelihood. He with his wife and one child came to Prince Edward Island in 1812. They were greatly disappointed with the appearance of things on the island, and Mrs. Davis says she cried nearly all the time they stayed there. After a year on the island Mr. Davis moved to Point de Bute. Although he was a small man and not accustomed to farm work, he remained in Point de Bute for ten years and made a good living for his increasing family. At the end of that time he got a grant of good land in Little Shemogue, on what is now called the Davis Road. On this land Mr. Davis put up a log house and moved his family there. After undergoing most of the privations incidental to such an experience, success came, and with is a comfortable and happy old age. In his later years Mr. Davis made a trip to his old home in England, and received a substantial legacy that awaited him there. He had a family of ten children, five sons and five daughters. Henry, the second son, was a member of the family at Prospect for fourteen years, and came to be looked upon almost as a son. John settled in Leicester, N.S., and was a successful farmer, with a large family. One son is a Methodist minister in the Nova Scotia Conference, and another is stipendiary magistrate for the town of Amherst.

Henry Davis was a miller, and settled first in Amherst. One of his sons, T. T. Davis, is a professor in a western College. The other sons of Daniel Davis were farmers, two of whom remained at the old home in Shemogue, where some of their descendants still live.

John Woods was another of the early emigrants who found his way to Prospect. He was a Manxman. After a time he bought a farm at Tidnish, N.S., and subsequently moved to the Gulf Shore, Wallace. Mr. Woods visited Prospect Farm in the seventies, and was greatly delighted to see the old place again.

Samson Clark was also a member of the family for a time. He was a brother of the late Alexander Clark, D.D. When he left Prospect he located on a farm on what he called the "Roadside," back of Amherst, N.S., now Salem. Samson, although a strong man physically, and with plenty of brains, did not make life a success. He became blind in his later years, and never prospered financially. Politically Mr. Clark would stand for a countryman of his who, when asked soon after landing in America what his politics were, answered, "Is there a government here?" He was told that there was. "Then," said he, "I'm ag'in the government."

Isaac Vandegrift came from Halifax to Point de Bute. His mother was a widow. He married Miriam Smith, from Sackville, and the ceremony took place at the "Brick House," Prospect. Isaac settled at Hall's Hill, but afterward moved back to Point de Bute. He was an excellent ploughman, and was one of the drovers north when the Richibucto and Miramichi markets were supplied with beef from the Westmoreland marshes. He contracted consumption and died comparatively young. Mrs. Edward Jones, of Point de Bute, is the only one of his five children now living.

A family named Ireland came to Prospect early in the centry, and Mr. Trueman took some trouble in assisting Mr. Ireland to locate. These entries are found in the journal: "May, 1811—Robert goes to Amherst for Mr. Ireland's goods," and, later, Mr. Trueman "goes with Mr. Ireland and Amos Fowler to Westcock for advice." Mr. Ireland moved to King's County, where he farmed for a time. Later he went to Ontario. The late Hon. George Ryan, when at Ottawa, met some members of the Ireland family and renewed old acquaintanceship after a separation of forty years.

## COLPITTS.

Extracts from the historical paper read at the re-union of the Colpitts family in Coverdale, Albert County, Sept. 6th, 1900:

"In the spring of 1783, immediately after the close of the Revolutionary War, there came to Halifax, from Newcastle-on-Tyne, England, a tall, stalwart Englishman with his wife and family of seven children. The name of the man was Robert Colpitts, as far as we know the only one of the name to come out from the Mother Country, and the progenitor of all on this side of the Atlantic who bear the name. What his occupation or position in society was before his emigration we can only conjecture. Strange to say, there does not exist a scrap of writing which throws any light on these questions, and tradition is almost equally at fault. Later in life Robert Colpitts was a captain of militia, and it is thought he had some connection with the army before his emigration. Whatever his occupation was he must have been possessed of some means, as among the articles brought from England were things which would be counted as luxuries rather than necessities for a new settler among the wilds of New Brunswick. For instance, among these articles were three large clocks.

"Tradition says that this was not his first visit to Canada. Before the outbreak of the American Revolution he had been over, it is believed, in connection with a survey of the Bay of Fundy.

At this time he had made a small clearing on what is now the Charles Trites' farm, in Coverdale, and put up a small cabin on the place. He then returned to Newcastle-on-Tyne, and closed up his business with the expectation of returning with his family. In the meantime the war between England and her American colonies had broken out, and he could not reach Nova Scotia until the trouble was settled, which was not for seven years. For a part of this time the family had charge of a toll bridge near Newcastle. The following incident is declared to have actually occurred while they were keeping the toll bridge. A large man, riding a very small donkey, one day came up to the bridge and asked the amount of the toll. The charge was more than he felt inclined to pay, so he asked what would it be for a man with a load. Finding that it was considerably less he at once laid down the smaller sum, picked up the donkey in his arms, and walked over the bridge. From Halifax Mr. Colpitts and the two oldest boys made their way overland, walking the most of the way from there to Moncton, while the others came in a vessel soon afterwards. When they reached Coverdale the land he had improved had been pre-empted, and Mr. Colpitts had to push on. He settled at Little River, five miles from its mouth."

The writer, after giving a fuller account of the family, says: "It is, we freely confess, the history of a race of humble farmers, and such, for the most part, have been their descendants; no one of the name has yet occupied a prominent place in the public life of our country. But the name has always been an honorable one, and those who have borne it have been, with few exceptions, honest, God-fearing, God-honoring men and women."

Mr. James Colpitts, of Point de Bute, is a great-grandson of Mr. Robert Colpitts.

## MONRO.

Alexander Monro was born in Banff, Scotland. His father, John Monro, and family came from Aberdeen to Miramichi, New Brunswick, in 1815. He remained in Miramichi three years and then moved to Bay Verte. The next move was to Mount Whatley, and, after a few years stay there, Mr. Monro purchased a wilderness lot on Bay Verte Road, to which they removed, and after years of strenuous labor made for themselves a comfortable home.

It was from Mr. Robert King, school master—referred to in another part of this book—that the son, Alexander Monro, received the inspiration and training that started him on the road to success in life. His biographer says: "When he was twenty-one years of age a Mr. Robert King came into the district to take charge of the school, and under his care young Monro studied in the winter evenings geometry, algebra and land surveying. Mr. King possessed a surveying compass, and gave him practical instruction in land surveying, leading him to decide to follow that business.

Mr. Monro obtained a recommendation from Dr. Smith, of Fort Cumberland, and others, and in the year 1837 went to Fredericton to obtain an appointment from the Hon. Thomas Baillie, then Surveyor-General of the Province. Mr. Baillie complimented him on his attainments, but refused to appoint him to the office. When Mr. Monro got back to St. John he had but two shillings in his pocket, and with this meagre sum he started on foot for home. Before he had gone far he found a job of masonry work and earned fifteen shillings. With this money he returned to St. John, and purchased Gibson's "Land Surveying" and some cakes for lunch, and set out again for Westmoreland. On the way he worked a day at digging potatoes, for which he received two shillings, and later on built a chimney and was paid two pounds.

The next year Mr. Monro received the appointment of Deputy Crown Land Surveyor. In 1848 he was made a Justice of the Peace, and was the surveyor to run the boundary line between Nova Scotia and New Brunswick. He was the author of a number of works, one on Land Surveying, also one on the "History, Geography and Productions of New Brunswick, Nova Scotia and Prince Edward Island." For a number of years he edited an educational monthly magazine called the *Parish School Advocate*. His biographer adds: "Such is the life and labors of one of our foremost and most useful citizens, and if there is a moral to be read from it, it is this, that to make a man of cultured tastes, a student, a scholar and a publicist of acknowledged rank and value in the country, universities with their libraries and endowments are not absolutely necessary; social position, influential connection and wealth are not necessary. Without such adventitious aids, what is wanted is a native taste for research and inquiry, and a determination of character superior to environment."

## PALMER—KNAPP.

The Palmers and Knapps were Loyalists. C. E. Knapp, a grandson of Loyalist Knapp, writes: "The largest part of Staten Island, New York, should have been the possession of the Palmers of Westmoreland. Their ancestor, John Palmer, who was by profession a lawyer, moved from New York to Staten Island. He had been appointed one of the first judges of the New York Court of Oyer and Terminer. He was also a member of the Governor's Council, and afterwards Sheriff. When the Revolutionary War broke out his son Gideon held the commission of captain in Delancy's Rangers, and when the war terminated he, in common with the other Loyalists, had to leave the country."

Together with his brother-in-arms, Titus Knapp, John Palmer found a new home at Old Fort Cumberland, where they commenced business as general traders. They purchased adjoining farms, and these still go by the name of the "Knapp and Palmer farms." Mr. Palmer afterwards moved to Dorchester Cape, induced to do so because it reminded him of his old home in New York. Palmer and Knapp must have found their loyalty expensive, as their confiscated property is now worth untold millions. In Mr. Knapp's case it was not so bad, as his property went to his half-brother, who, fortunately for him, was a Quaker and did not "fight."

The Palmers have taken a prominent place in the history of New Brunswick.

Mr. Gideon Palmer, a son of Gideon (first), was one of the successful shipbuilders of Dorchester in the fifties, and Philip, another son, was for some years a member of the New Brunswick Legislature. The late Judge Palmer, of St. John, was a son of Philip Palmer.

Charles E. Knapp, barrister, of Dorchester, is clerk of the Probate Courty, and one of the oldest practising lawyers of Westmoreland. Mr. Titus Knapp represented the county for some time in the Legislature of New Brunswick, and for many years did a large trading business at Westmoreland Point.

## HARPER.

Christopher Harper was born in a small village near Hull, in Yorkshire. He emigrated to Nova Scotia in 1774, bringing his family and his nephew, Thomas King, with him. He arrived at Fort Cumberland on a fine day in May, and his surprise was great the next morning to see the ground covered with snow. Mr. Harper bought a property to the south-east of the garrison lands, and moved his family into a house said to have been built by the Acadians; but this is very doubtful, as these people chose to burn their dwellings rather than let them fall into the hands of the English. Tradition says Mr. Harper brought stock, both horses and cattle, with him from Yorkshire.

In 1777 Mr. Harper's house and barn were burned by the Eddy rebels, and soon after the Loyalists came to Nova Scota he sold his property at the fort to his son-in-law, Gideon Palmer, and moved to Sackville, having purchased land near Morris's Mills. It is said he came into possession of this property through prosecuting one Ayer and others for setting fire to his buildings at Fort Cumberland. In 1809 he obtained a grant from the Government at Fredericton of the mill-pond, and some two hundred or three hundred acres of wilderness land in Sackville, including about forty acres of marsh on the east side of the Tantramar River, above Coles's Island.

Mr. Harper had three sons and four daughters. His son Christopher, who was a captain in the army in early life, left for Quebec, via Richibucto and Miramichi, and was not heard from after leaving Miramichi. John married Miss Thornton (whose father was a Loyalist), and after living at the mill for a time moved to Dorchester. William married Phoebe Haliday, from Cobequid, and built on the place where I. C. Harper, of Sackville, now lives; Catherine married Gideon Palmer; Annie married Major Richard Wilson, a north of Ireland man; Fannie married Thomas King, and Charlotte married Bedford Boultonhouse.

Christopher Harper owned the first two-wheeled chaise that was run in Westmoreland County. He was a magistrate and used to solemnize marriage, and sometimes officiated in the Church of England in the absence of the rector.

The Harpers of Sackville and Bay Verte are descendants of the two brothers, William and John.

## ETTER—WETHERED.

The Etters and Wethereds were on the Isthmus very shortly after 1755. I find that Samuel Wethered was married to Dorothy Eager, Nov. 26th, 1761, by license from the Government. Dorothy Eager was a Scotch lass from Dumfries. Mrs. Atkinson, a grand-daughter, has several pieces of fancy needlework done by Mrs. Wethered. "Sarah Huston Wethered was born at Cumberland, in the Province of Nova Scotia, June 10th, 1763, at ten o'clock in the morning. Joshua Winslow Wethered was born at Cumberland, Nova Scotia, in September, 1764, at ten o'clock in the evening."

Peter Etter was a jeweller and silversmith, and kept a shop near Fort Cumberland. He married Letitia Patton, daughter of Mark Patton, and was brother-in-law to Colonel John Allan. Peter Etter was twice married, his second wife being Sarah Wethered. He was lost at sea in coming from Boston to Cumberland. His widow became the second wife of Amos Fowler, of Fowler's Hill. Peter Etter (second) married Elizabeth Wethered, and settled at Westmoreland, and had a family of nine children, Bradley, Peter, Joshua, Letitia, George, Maria, Samuel, James, and Margaret.

The Etters are large marsh owners on the Aulac, and the aboideau across that river takes its name—the Etter Aboideau—from Peter Etter, who was one of the principal promoters of that work.

I find Jonathan Eddy's name among the customers of jeweller Etter. Mr. Eddy's watch must have been like that of Artemus Ward's or he must have been agent for others, judging from the amount of money he annually paid for repairs.

The Etters were originally from Switzerland, and were engaged in making glass before coming to this country.

## CAHILL.

John R. Cahill was born in London, England, in the year 1777. His father was a ship-owner, but decided to educate his son for the Church. During a college vacation young Cahill was sent as supercargo in one of his father's ships bound for Halifax. On the return voyage the vessel was wrecked on the coast of Nova Scotia. All on board, however, were rescued and brought back to Halifax. For reasons not now known, Mr. Cahill remained on this side of the Atlantic and engaged for a time in teaching school. He married Miss Lesdernier, a sister of Mrs. Richard John Uniacke, and settled in Sackville as a farmer. They had a family of eleven, and Mr. Cahill received regular remittances from his father's estate as long as he lived. Because of his superior education he was often called upon by his neighbors to assist in transacting business of various kinds. Mr. Cahill died in 1852. The late John E. Cahill, of Westmoreland Point, was a son, and Walter Cahill, stipendiary magistrate of Sackville, a grandson, of John R. Cahill.

## SMITH.

There were two John Smiths who came from Yorkshire and settled at Chignecto in the decade between 1770 and 1780.

One settled in Fort Lawrence and married Miss Chapman. The Smiths of Fort Lawrence and Shinemicas are descendants of this family. William Smith of Albert County, who married Parmelia Trueman, was of this family.

The other John Smith settled near Fort Cumberland, but remained only a short time. He incurred the enmity of some of the outlaws in the neighborhood, and as a result had his buildings burned, in one of which a large quantity of goods was stored that he had brought to the country. This so discouraged him that he left the place and settled at Newport, N.S. David Smith, of Amherst, belongs to this family.

## OULTON.

Charles Oulton, the first of the name to settle on the Isthmus, came to Nova Scotia with his mother in 1759. At this time Mrs. Oulton was a widow, but before she had been here long she married Capt. Sennacherib Martyn. Capt. Martyn had been with Winslow at the capture of Beausejour.

Young Oulton was seventeen years old when he landed at Halifax. Shortly after this he came to Cumberland, and his name is on the list of the first grantees of Cumberland Township, in 1763. He settled in Jolicure on the farm now in possession of Joseph D. Wells; here, no doubt, his grant was located.

Charles Oulton married a Miss Fillimore, and they had a family of twelve children, seven daughters and five sons. The children's names were: William, Charles, Thomas, George, Jane, Sally, Patience, Mary, Charity, Abigal, Betsy, and a twelfth, who died young.

William married a Miss Smith; Thomas a Miss Trenholm; George a Miss King; Charity a Mr. Williams, of Fredericton; Abigal a Mr. Tingley, of Albert County, N.B.; Mary a Mr. Frank Siddall; Patience a Mr. Smith; Jane also married a Mr. Smith; Sarah a Mr. Fields; Betsy a Mr. Bulmer. A daughter of Mrs. Williams married a Mr. Fisher, also of Fredericton, and they had five sons: Edwin, Henry, George, Peter, and the late Judge Fisher.

George, the youngest son, inherited the homestead in Jolicure, and was for many years one of the leading men in the parish. He married Miss King, of Westmoreland Point, by whom he had three sons: Thomas E., Cyrus, and Rufus. Squire Oulton, as George was usually called, was one of the most genial of men. In figure he was tall and straight. He had an open countenance, a quick step, a hearty laugh, and a pleasant "good morning" for everyone. He was just the kind of man to make friends. He enjoyed a good honest horse-race, and was always ready to bet a beaver hat on any test question that gave a chance of settlement in that way. An incident is told of him in connection with a trip made by his son Cyrus, which gives one a good idea of the man. It was customary before the days of railroads for the farmers and traders in Westmoreland to send teams loaded with produce as far north as Miramichi. These trips were generally made in the early winter, and butter, cheese, woolen cloth, socks, mittens, etc., found a ready market. The journey usually lasted ten days or more. Cyrus was sent by his father, Squire Oulton, on one of these journeys. A storm delayed the party, and more than the usual time was consumed before the return. When Cyrus returned he was not particularly prompt in reporting the success of the transaction to headquarters. At last his father asked him about the returns, and Cyrus said: "Well, to tell you the truth, father, I did not bring any money back with me. I met a number of good fellows and had to stand my share with the others, and the money is all gone." There was silence for a minute and then the Squire replied, "That is right, Cyrus, always be a man among men." That was the last of the affair, but it is porbably that Mr. Oulton chose some other agent to market the next load of produce.

In later years Cyrus used to enjoy telling the following story, based on one of his boyish experiences: "His father had been trying to buy a pari of cattle from Mr. Harper, in Sackville. They could not agree on the price, and Mr. Oulton had come away without purchasing. The next day he decided to send Cyrus over to get the oxen, with instructions to offer Mr. Harper twenty seven pounds for them, but if he would not take it, to give him twenty-eight. Cyrus started away on horseback, in great spirits,full of the importance of his mission. He rode as quickly as possible to Mr. Harper's, and as soon as he saw that gentleman delivered at once his full instructions, that his father wanted the cattle, and if he would not take twenty-seven pounds for them he would give him twenty-eight. Cyrus got the cattle, but not for twenty-seven pounds."

The Oulton nameis largely represented inJolicure at the present time, and most of those who bear it are energetic, industrious, and successful farmers. A few of the name have tried other professions and have succeeded. Geo. J. Oulton, Principal of the Moncton Schools, and one of the most capable teachers in the Province, is a Jolicure boy, and a descendant of Charles Oulton.

## KEILLOR.

Thomas Keillor came to Nova Scotia from Skelton, Yorkshire, in 1774. His wife's maiden name was Mary Thompson. He settled near Fort Cumberland, on the farm now known as the "Fowler homestead."

Mr. Keillor had five children—three sons, John, Thomas and Thompson, and two daughters, Elizabeth and Ann. John married a Miss Weldon and settled in Dorchester, where he and his descendants occupied a prominent place for many years. The name became extinct in that parish in 1899 at the death of Mrs. Thomas Keillor.

Thomas married a Miss Trenholm and settled at Amherst Point. He had a number of sons. Several of the family moved to Ontario. Robert married a Miss Dobson and remained on the homestead. His descendants still own the farm at Amherst Point. Coates married a Miss Jones and settled at Upper Miramichi. One of Coates's sons moved to Upper Canada, and the name is still found there. Some of the descendants, but none of the name, now live in Point de Bute.

Thompson died when a young man from a severe cold caught while hauling wood from the lakes. Ann married Amos Fowler, and Elizabeth married William

Trueman, as stated in another place.

The Keillors were men of integrity, with a good deal of combativeness in their make up, and not noted for polished address. The following story is told of one of the Keillor boys: One morning when taking a load of port to the fort, at the time the Eddy rebels were at Camp Hill, he was met by a young man on horseback. The young man, after eliciting from Mr. Keillor where he was taking the pork, ordered him to turn about and take it to the rebel camp. This Mr. Keillor refused to do point blank. In the parley and skirmish that followed Mr. Keillor managed to dehorse his man, bind him on the sled, and forthwith delivered him safely at the fort with his carcasses of pork. The young man proved to be Richard John Uniacke, who afterwards became one of the most celebrated of Nova Scotia's public men. In after years, when Mr. Uniacke had become Attorney-General of Nova Scotia, and able lawyer, and a good loyal subject, he was conducting a case in the Amherst Court-house. This same Mr. Keillor was called forward as a witness, and during the cross-examination, when things were probably getting a little uncomfortable for the witness, he ventured to say to Mr. Uniacke:

"I think we have met before, sir."

Mr. Uniacke replied rather haughtily, "You have the advantage of me, I believe."

"And it is not the first time I have had the advantage of you," replied Mr. Keillor.

"When was this?" asked Mr. Uniacke, in a tone that showed how fully he considered himself the master of the situation.

Mr. Keillor replied, "At the time of the rebellion, when I delivered you, a rebel and a prisoner, to the fort along with my pork."

It is said that the Attorney-General left the further conduct of the case to his subordinates.

Thomas, the brother who settled in Amherst, was once warned as a juryman to attend court, to be held in a building little better than a barn. When Mr. Keillor was chosen on a cause, and came forward to the desk to be sworn, he refused absolutely to take the oath. When remonstrated with, he said, "I will never consent to hold the King's Court in a barn." And this juryman, who was so zealous of the King's honor, was allowed to have his own way. The outcome of this was that soon after the county erected at Amherst a suitable building for a court-house.

## WARD.

The name Ward was early on the Isthmus. Nehemiah was one of the first grantees of Cumberland. Jonathan Ward, the first to settle in Point de Bute, came from New England in 1760. It is said his coming to this country was occasioned by his falling in love with a young lady whose parents objected to his becoming their son-in-law. The lady, however, was willing to accept her lover without the parents' consent. An elopement was planned and carried out, the young couple coming to Cumberland to set up housekeeping. Mrs. Ward did not live very long after her marriage, and left a young daughter. This daughter was twice married, first to a Mr. Reynolds, and after his death to an Englishman named Merrill. From this union came the Merrills of Sackville, a name quite common in that parish seventy-five years ago, but now extinct.

Jonathan Ward married, as his second wife, Tabitha — —-, a young woman who accompanied his first wife when she left her home in New Haven. They settled in Upper Point de Bute, and lived to a great age, Mr. Ward being ninety-six at his death. Stephen, the only son, inherited the home place and married a Miss Folsom. The Folsoms were from New York, and one of them came to Prince Edward Island to attend to business for the firm. While there he married. Soon after this event Mr. Folsom seems to have been caught by the land craze that few men escaped at that date, and got a large grant of land in Antigonishe County, Nova Scotia. Before they got fairly settled in their new home, Mrs. Folsom died, leaving a daughter. Mr. Folsom soon after left his grant of land and with his little daughter came to Fort Cumberland. Leaving her with friends he went away and was never heard of again. It was supposed he was lost at sea.

The Wards were originally from Wales. Of Stephen Ward's family, Henry and William settled at Point de Bute, and Nathaniel at Wood Point, N.B.

## DICKSON.

Major Thomas Dickson, the first of the name on the Isthmus, was one of the New England soldiers present at the taking of Fort Beausejour in 1755. The family were originally from the north of Ireland, and emigrated to the old colonies.

Major Dickson served under General Amherst, and his family had in their possession up to a few years ago a document in which General Amherst commissioned Major Dickson to do certain work that necessitated great risk and skill if it were to be successful.

Thomas Dickson's name is on the list of the first grantees of Cumberland Township, and he received a grant of a large block of land about a mile above Point de Bute Corner, on which he afterward settled. He married a Miss Wethered, and had a family of ten children—James, Dalton, Thomas, Charles, John, Robert, Nancy, Mary, Sarah, and Catherine. Mary married a Mr. Harper, Nancy a Mr. Gleanie, Sarah a brother of Col. John Allan, and after his death Thomas Roach, Esq., of Fort Lawrence; James married Susanna Dickson, and remained on the homestead. Of the other sons, Thomas Law settled in Amherst and represented the county for some years in the Provincial Legislature; Robert, Charles and John entered the British navy. John was shot in an engagement in the English Channel. Robert was drowned in Shelburne Harbor. His vessel was lying in the stream, and he, while in the town, laid a wager that he could swim to the ship. He attempted it, but lost his life in the effort. Charles left the navy and settled in Machias, where he left a large family.

Shortly before the capture of Quebec, Major Dickson was sent out from Fort Cumberland to disperse a band of Acadians who had been reported by one of their number as camping near the Jolicure Lakes with the object of raiding the settlers.

The Major with his men started out in pursuit, the Frenchman acting as guide. The camp was found deserted, and the party started on the return home. When they reached the Le Coup stream, an affluent of the Aulac, they found the tide had risen so much that they were unable to proceed farther in that direction, so turning to the left, they followed the main stream to where there was a crossing. While preparing to ford the stream they were suddenly fired upon by the Acadians, who were in hiding behind the dyke. All the party were killed save Major Dickson and the Acadian guide. Both were made prisoners, and as soon as the woods was reached the Acadian was scalped and the Englishman was told that he "must walk alone."

Then starting north they made only necessary stops until they reached Three Rivers, in Quebec. Here the Major was handed over to the French officer in charge at that place, and was put under guard, but treated well, as had been the case on the journey from Nova Scotia. Possibly roasted muskrat would not be considered an appetizing diet, but the major found it kept away hunger, and that was no small consideration in a journey of five hundred miles without a commissariat department.

The prisoner had not been many days at Three Rivers when he received word that Quebec had been taken by the English, and he was again a free man. He soon made his way back to Fort Cumberland, and was present at the defence of the fort during the attack of the Eddy rebels and did good service on that day.

The Dicksons were men who thought for themselves. James, a son of the first James, was a teacher for a time, and in his later years did all the conveyancing in the neighborhood, such as the writing of deeds and wills. He was an omnivorous reader, and, like Silas Wegg, was inclined to "drop into poetry." Some of his efforts in this direction on local happening caught the ear and had the ring that stirred the emotions. Titus, the only grandson of the major, lives on the old farm, and though eighty-three years of age, is still vigorous in mind. The writer is indebted to him for some of the facts given in this sketch.

## ATKINSON.

There were two Atkinson families that came to Nova Scotia about the year 1774, one from Middlesex, the other from Yorkshire.

The Middlesex family settled in Fort Lawrence. Capt. S. B. Atkinson, a descendant of this family, writes: "My great-grandfather was a man of considerable substance in the County of Middlesex, England, known as gentleman farmer, and dubbed "Esquire." The tradition is he married a Lord's daughter, whose title would be Lady — —-, and as her family would not recognize either her or her husband, they left the country in disgust."

Mr. Atkinson came to Nova Scotia alone in 1774, and prospected the province. It was a beautiful summer and autumn, and he was delighted with the country. After securing a grant of land in Fort Lawrence, in the old Township of Cumberland, he returned to England and made arrangements to move his family to his new domain the following spring. To accomplish this he chartered the good ship

*Arethusa,* and put on board of her his family and farm tenants, all of his belongings, household goods, and farming utensils, and after his safe arrival in Nova Scotia, located on what is now known as the Torry Bent farm.

Capt. Atkinson, in his letter, gives some interesting information relative to the family after settling in this country. He says: "My grand-father's name was Robert. He was the sailor of the family. He served his apprenticeship to the sea out of England, and followed his father to America, sailing as master prior to 1800." His wife was Sarah, daughter of Obediah Ayer, generally known as Commodore Ayer, noted Yankee rebel, one of two brothers from Massachusetts.

Mr. Ayer held an officer's commission in Washington's army in 1776 and was also Commodore of a privateer out of Boston in 1812. In consideration of his service in the war of 1776, the United States Government gave him a grant of land in Ohio, at that time one of the territories. Some years ago his heirs undertook to look up the records, but found they had been burned in the Capitol during the War of 1812. "Only for that little incident," Capt. Atkinson says, "I might have owned the site where Cleveland now stands or otherwise—probably otherwise."

For services in 1812 Commodore Ayer was granted a pension, but died before any payments were made to him. His nearest connections, however, received two hundred dollars a year as long they lived (sic).

Capt. Robert Atkinson sailed his last voyage, from Kingston to Jamaica, in 1804, and died at that port of yellow fever. His widow returned to Sackville, leaving her son Edwin, their only child, with his grandfather in Fort Lawrence, where he remained until he was twenty-one years of age.

Mr. Atkinson had three sons besides Robert, who lived with him in Fort Lawrence. Thomas moved to Kent County, where his descendants still live. William and John remained in Fort Lawrence, and the Atkinsons there now are descended from these brothers. Capt. Stephen Atkinson, from whom most of the information about the family has been obtained, is a master mariner, and has commanded some fine ships in his day. He has now given up the sea and spends a part of his time in Sackville.

The Atkinson family from Yorkshire settled first at River Hebert, Cumberland County, N.S. Robert was the founder of the family. He did not remain in River Hebert for any length of time, but purchased a farm in Sackville, and moved his family there. This farm was afterwards sold by his son Christopher, and is now the site of the Mount Allison educational institutions.

Robert was married and had three children when he came to Nova Scotia. He was twice married, and was the father of fourteen children. Thomas, Christopher, Elizabeth, Sallie, Joseph, Robert, William, John and Stephen were the names of the first family. Several of the sons settled in Sackville. Christopher, after selling his property in Sackville, purchased a farm in Point de Bute, and moved to that place. He had a large family of boys. Robert (second) moved to Shediac. One brother went to the United States and joined the Latter-Day Saints. Joseph married Ann Campbell, the daughter of Lieutenant Campbell, a Waterloo soldier, and settled at Wood Point. They had ten children, six sons and four daughters. Isaac, Nelson,

Hance, William and Joseph all became master mariners, and were fine navigators. Woe be to the sailor who fell into their hands and did not know his duty or refused to perform it!

The family still have in their possession their ancestor Campbell's sword and some other relics belonging to the old soldier.

The Atkinsons have always been a strong, vigorous and self-reliant family, and have made a good record in this new country.

## LOWERISON.

The following information regarding the Lowerisons was secured chiefly from Robert Lowerison, of Sackville, a great-grandson of the first Richard Lowerison.

Richard Lowerison, the first to come to America, was born in Yorkshire, England, in the year 1741, and married Mary Grey in 1762. Ten years later Mr. Lowerison sailed from Liverpool, Eng., bound for Halifax, where he landed on the 1st of May. He settled on the Petitcodiac River, in Westmoreland County, N.B., but the frequent raids made by the Eddy rebels in that district caused him to purchase and remove to a farm adjoining the western bounds of the Garrison lands of Fort Cumberland. The buildings first erected by him have long since disappeared. The farm has been occupied by his son Thomas, by his grandson James, and at present by William Miner.

Six children survived Richard and Mary Grey Lowerison—Elizabeth, who married William Doncaster, and settled at Amherst Point; Anne, who married John Carter, and settled east of Fort Cumberland; Thomas, who married Hannah Carter, and occupied the homestead; Richard, who married Abigail Merrill, and after spending twelve years between the old home, Amherst Point, and Mapleton, moved to Frosty Hollow, Sackville, on September 18th, 1817, on the farm now occupied by his son, Thomas Lowerison, and his grandson, Bradford Carter; Joseph, the third son of Richard, married Mary Siddall and settled near Mount Whatley, about two miles from the homestead. Mary married James Carter, who for a time kept a public house in Dorchester, but afterwards moved to Amherst, Nova Scotia.

Richard Lowerison and his wife attended the Methodist church in Point de Bute, as may be seen in the deed given by William Chapman to John Wesley. He acted as precentor in the old stone "Meeting House." He died February 24th, 1825, and was buried in the Point de Bute Cemetery. Mary Grey Lowerison, born in the East Riding of Yorkshire, England, died September 16th, 1834, and lies beside her husband.

Mr. Lowerison must have had some means when he came to the country, for while living near Fort Cumberland he did an extensive business in sending beef cattle to Halifax. His partner for a time was a man named Rice. He seems first to have deceived Mr. Lowerison, and then robbed him by running away with the proceeds of three droves of cattle, leaving Mr. Lowerison accountable for the cattle, with no cash on hand to meet the bills. The worry from this affected his mind to such an extent that he never fully recovered. The Lowerison name, until quite recently, was pronounced as if spelled Lawrence. The family has not increased greatly in the new country. Although the sons had large families, there are very few grandchildren. Robert Lowerison, of Sackville, is the only living member of a large family. Captain Richard Lowerison, of Amherst, is a descendant. Captain Thomas, Joseph, and Siddall, grandsons of Richard, represent the name at Westmoreland Point.

The Lowerisons were always understood to be men of their word.

## FILLIMORE.

John Fillimore came from New England to Fort Lawrence, N.S., in 1763 and soon after settled in Jolicure. He had a number of sons, two of whom, John and Spiller, settled at home—John on the homestead, and Spiller on an adjoining farm.

At the close of the Revolutionary War, Spiller sold his farm and returned to the United States. John married Jemima Tingley, of Sackville, and had a family of twelve children. W. C. Fillimore, of Westmoreland Point, and Lewis Fillimore, of Amherst, are grandsons of John.

The Fillimores came originally from Manchester, England, to Long Island, New York. Captain John, father of John, who came to Nova Scotia, was once commissioned by the State of Connecticut to clear the coast of pirates, who were causing a good deal of trouble at the time. So well did Captain Fillimore perform the duty that the town of Norwich presented him with a handsome cane as a mark of their appreciation of his services. This cane is still in possession of the family.

The Fillimores are a long-lived race of men, and have shown themselves well able to hold their own in the competition of life. The name has given a president to the United States.

## MINER.

Sylvanus Miner, the first of the name on the Isthmus, was of New England stock. He and Robert King, "Schoolmaster King," as he was generally called, came from Windsor on foot to Mount Whatley, N.B., about 1810. Mr. Miner's father died when he was a boy, and his mother apprenticed her son to a blacksmith. His mother was a Miss Brownell, of Jolicure.

When young Miner had completed his apprenticeship he came to Jolicure by invitation to see his uncle, and afterwards settled at Mount Whatley. He was twice married. His first wife was a Miss Church, of Fort Lawrence; his second, Miss Styles, from Truro, N.S. The sons, James, William and Nathan, now represent the name at Mount Whatley. Mr. Miner was an upright man, and successful in his business of blacksmith and farmer.

## DOBSON.

The Dobsons were among the first of Yorkshire emigrants to arrive in Nova Scotia. There were two brothers, George and Richard. George brought with him a wife and grown-up family. His daughter Margaret was married to William Wells before the family left England. Richard was a bachelor, and tradition says he had been a soldier. George purchased a farm in Upper Point de Bute. Neither of the brothers lived long in their new home. Richard died in February, 1773, and George in July of the same year. George's will is dated the 24th July, 1773, and is recorded the 24th November by John Huston. It is witnessed by Mark Patten and J. Allen.

George had four sons, George, David, Richard and John, and two unmarried daughters, Elizabeth and Mary. George and John settled at Point de Bute. Richard sold his share of the homestead to John in 1795, and moved to Cape Tormentine, where he secured a large tract of land and became one of the substantial men of the place. A large number of his descendants are in that locality at the present time. The Dobsons, of Cape Breton, N.S., are descendants of Richard. John sold his farm and moved to Sussex, King's Co., N.B. George Dobson, of Sussex, is a grandson of John. David went to Halifax. George remained on the homestead at Point de Bute, and the Dobsons of Jolicure are descendants of George by his son Abraham.

Mrs. Dobson, the widow of George (first) married a Mr. Falkinther. He did not live long, and Mrs. Falkinther, who was said to be a very fine looking woman, had one of her grand-daughters to live with her during the last years of her life. Her grandchildren called her "Grandmother Forkey."

"Old Abe," as Abraham was familiarly called, was a character in his day. He used to make annual and sometimes semi-annual trips to St. John to dispose of his butter and farm products, and was the kind of man to get all the enjoyment out of these journeys that was in them. It was said that he had large feet, and that early in life one of them was run over by a cart wheel, making it larger than the other. One day, while sitting in a St. John hotel, with the smaller foot forward, a man, noticing the size of it, said, "I will make a bet that that is the largest foot in the city." "Done," said Old Abe. The bet was made, when Mr. Dobson brought forward the other foot and won the wager.

Abraham was one of the best farmers in the township. He named his eldest son Isaac, and had Isaac name his eldest son Jacob. Perhaps the likeness to the old patriarch ended here. He had a large family of boys, to all of whom he gave farms. His youngest son, Robert, was drowned in the Missiquash Valley one December morning as he was skating to his farm on the Bay Verte Road.

The Dobsons were good men for a new country, and did not take life too seriously. Jacob, Frank, Alder, Alonzo and John Dobson and their families represent the name now in Jolicure. Dr. Gay Dobson, of Poughkeepsie, N.Y., U.S., is a descendant. John, a brother of Abraham Dobson, left no sons.

## JONES.

William Jones came from Wales. He was one of the first settlers at Point de Bute Corner. He married Mary Dobson, a daughter of George Dobson. They had a large family. Ruth, their youngest daughter, married Stephen Goodwin and lived on the homestead. Stephen Goodwin came from St. John to Point de Bute with his mother, who was a widow. She subsequently became the second wife of Christopher Atkinson. By this marriage she had three sons, George, Abel and Busby, and one daughter, Nancy, who became the wife of John Fawcett, Esq., of Upper Sackville. J. H. Goodwin, of Point de Bute, is a son of Stephen Goodwin.

## TINGLEY.

Palmer Tingley emigrated from Kingston-on-the-Thames to Malden, Mass., in 1666. Josiah Tingley, a descendant, came to Sackville, N.B., in 1763. William, a grandson of Josiah Tingley, married Elizabeth Horton and settled in Point de Bute in 1794. He bought land from Josiah B. Throop. The witnesses to the deed were Joseph and Ichabod Throop. Like most of the early settlers, Mr. Tingley raised a large family, and all his sons became farmers. Four of them, John, Harris, Caleb, and William, settled near their father. Josiah settled in Jolicure, Joshua at Shemogue, and Isaac at Point Midgie. There were four daughters. Ann married Joseph Irving, of Tidnish; Mary, Cyrus McCully, Amherst, N.S.; Helener, William McMorris, of Great Shemogue; and Margaret, Asa Read, also of Shemogue. There were eleven children in all, and their longevity will surely bear comparison with that of any family in Canada, and is well worth recording:

John Tingley, born 1794, died 1874, aged 80.

Harris Tingley, born 1795, died 1875, aged 80.

Joshua Tingley, born 1797, died 1897, aged 100.

William Tingley, born 1799, died 1868, aged 69.

Ann Tingley, born 1801, died 1881, aged 80.

Mary Tingley, born 1803, died 1890, aged 87.

Josiah Tingley, born 1807, died 1888, aged 81.

Helener Tingley, born 1809, still living in 1902, aged 93.

Isaac Tingley, born 1812, died 1891, aged 79.

Margaret Tingley, born 1816, still living in 1902, aged 86.

Caleb Tingley, born 1805, died 1880, aged 75.

The Tingleys are generally adherents of the Baptist Church. Robert, Obed, Harvey, William, Alfred and Err are grandsons of William Tingley and represent the name in Point de Bute and Jolicure.

## SIDDALL.

Ralph Siddall came from Yorkshire to Nova Scotia in 1772, and soon after, in company with Richard Lowerison, settled at "The Bend," now the town of Moncton, N.B. The Eddy rebels proving too strong in that locality for the loyal Englishmen, they soon returned to the protection of Fort Cumberland, and eventually settled near the fort. Mr. Siddall had a family of five children—two sons, Ralph and Francis, and three daughters. The daughters married, respectively: Thomas Carter, — —-Cook, and James Deware. The Dewares of Jolicure belong to his family. Ralph (second) married — —-Ayer and had two sons, Edward and William and three daughters. William settled on Gray's Road, near Wallace. Edward remained on the homestead. One of the daughters married Joseph Lowerison, another Ephraim Rayworth; one remained single. Francis Siddall settled first on the farm now owned by James Colpitts, near Point de Bute Corner, and married Mary Oulton, by whom he had a family of five children, Ralph, Stephen, Charles, Susan and Experience. Susan was twice married—first to Mariner Teed, of Dorchester, N.B., second, to Hugh McLeod. The late John Teed, of Dorchester, was a son of Mariner and Susan Teed. Experience married William Copp, of Bay Verte Road. The Copps were from New England, and settled first in Jolicure. Hiram, Harvey and Silas Copp, of Sackville, Albert and George, of Bay Verte, are sons of William Copp.

Ralph Siddall (third) married Susan Oulton and remained on the homestead at Westmoreland Point, which he named "The Crow's Nest." Mrs. Siddall is now living, at the age of eighty-six. Charles married Louisa Chappell, of Bay Verte, and is still living, at the ripe age of ninety-two years. Godfrey and Bill, of Bay Verte, N.B., and Charles, of Sackville, are his sons. Stephen married a Miss Brown and had a large family. His youngest son, George, is the only one living in the vicinity of the old home. Stephen had a remarkable memory, and greatly enjoyed a good sermon. He followed the sea for a number of years. After settling down at home, near Fort Cumberland, he was appointed to an office in the Customs, which he held to his death. Few men could tell a story better than Capt. Stephen Siddall.

## BROWNELL.

Rev. J. H. Brownell writes: "The present Brownell family are unable to tell definitely when their grandfather came to this country, but I find it recorded in 'A Biographical Sketch of the Loyalists,' by Lorenzo Sabine, in Vol. I, which I have by me, that in the year 1783 two brothers came from Vermont to New Brunswick. Joshua Brownell went to St. John, and Jeremiah came to Westmoreland, and settled in Jolicure. He married Annie Copp. They were the parents of nine children. Their names, etc., are as follows: Aaron married first, Vinie Dixon; they had one girl. His second wife was Margaret Weldon; they had two sons and five daughters. He settled in Dorchester. John married Eunice Polly; they had two sons and seven daughters. He settled in Jolicure. Jeremiah married Rebecca Dixon; they had seven sons and six daughters. He settled in Northport, N.S. Thomas never married, and lived in Jolicure. William married Annie Davis; they had five sons and five daughters. He settled in Northport, N.S. Sarah married Thomas Weldon. They lived in Jolicure for a time, and then moved away. When Weldon died Sarah came back and lived with Thomas. She had six children, one son and five daughters. Edward married Margaret Adams; they had thirteen children. He settled in Jolicure. Annie married George Church; they lived in Fort Lawrence, and had four sons and five daughters. Lovinia married Jesse Church, and lived in Point de Bute for a time, then moved to Amherst. They had five sons and seven daughters."

My information, up to the receipt of this letter, was very positive that Jeremiah Brownell came to Nova Scotia in 1763, with the Fillimores and others, landing at Fort Lawrence. The family were adherents of the Presbyterian Church, and took an active part in building and sustaining that church in Jolicure. The name has given two ministers to the denomination, Rev. J. H. Brownell, of Little Shemogue, N.B., and Rev. Hiram Brownell, of Northport, N.S.

## KING.

Thomas King came from a small village near Hull, Yorkshire, with his uncle, Christopher Harper, in 1773. Before starting for America Mr. Harper hired his nephew, who was a blacksmith, to work for him for three years for forty pounds sterling. When Mr. Harper found wages were high in this country, he released his nephew from the bargain, and young King worked several years in the Government Armory at Fort Cumberland. He married his cousin, Miss Harper, and they were the parents of six children, one son and five daughters. The son, Thomas, married a Miss Chandler; Jane married George Oulton; Fanny Thomas Bowser; one remained single; of the remaining two, one married Otho Read, and the other Jesse Read. Thomas King (second) owned a large farm that joined the Garrison land. He had a family of two daughters and four sons, Jane, — —-, Watson, Edward, James and Samuel. None of the sons, and but one of the daughters married. Edward and Samuel occupy the old place, and are the only members of the family now living. The "King boys," as they were called, were well read and good conversationalists. James was a school-teacher in his early years, and had a local reputation as a mathematician.

## RYAN.

Daniel Ryan came from Ireland to Nova Scotia soon after the Expulsion, and settled near Point de Bute corner. He married a Miss Henry. They had a family of eight—Daniel, Henry, James, William, and four daughters. One daughter married Joseph Black, of Dorchester, N.B.; another married a Mr. McBride; another, William Trenholm, of Point de Bute. William settled in Little Shemogue; Henry moved to Hastings, Cumberland, N.S.; James married Christina Forster, of Fort Lawrence, and lived for a time on the old place. About 1813 he moved to Millstream, King's Co., N.B., where the family for many years occupied a prominent place in public affairs.

## OGDEN.

The Ogdens were U. E. Loyalists. John (first) came from Long Island, New York, in 1790, and settled in Sackville, N.B., on the farm owned by the late Bloomer Ogden. An uncle of John Ogden spent the latter part of his life in prison rather than swear allegiance to the United States. John married Nancy Fawcett, a daughter of Mr. John Fawcett, Sackville, and had eight children—John, William, Henry, Thomas, Bloomer, Robert, Ann and Jane.

John (second) settled in Port Elgin. Edward Ogden, of Sackville, is a son of John. Amos and William of the same place are sons of Henry. The late Henry Ogden, of Jolicure, was connected with this family.

## TOWNSEND.

John Townsend came from Prince Edward Island and settled in Upper Jolicure early in the last century. His descendants are living there now. The Townsends are of English descent.

## ROBINSON.

The Robinsons were an English family that settled in Cornwallis, N.S., about 1780. Edmund Robinson, a son, removed to Parrsboro'. His wife was Miss Rand, a relative of the Rev. Silas Rand, the Micmac missionary. John Robinson of Point de Bute is a grandson of Edmund Robinson.

## PHALEN.

John Phalen came early to this country. He was educated for Holy Orders, but never entered the Church as one of its ministers. He was married in Halifax, and taught school in Point de Bute for a number of years. His son, John C. Phalen, was a member of the home of Thomas Trueman, of Point de Bute. John married Priscilla Goodwin, of Bay Verte, and had a large family. He settled at Bay Verte. John Phalen, of Amherst, is son of John C. Phalen. The Phalens of Westmoreland and Cumberland Counties are descendants of John. One of the name is in the Methodist ministry.

## WILLIAM DAVIDSON.

William Davidson came from Dumfries, Scotland, to this country in company with James Amos, in 1820. Mr. Amos landed at Charlottetown, but afterwards settled on the Murray Road, Botsford, and Mr. Davidson on the Bay Verte Road, alongside of John Monro. The Davidsons were a most intelligent family. The late Hugh Davidson of Tidnish was a member of this family and the Davidson brothers of Tidnish are sons of Hugh and William.

## TURNER.

William Turner, who settled in Bay Verte Road, came from the United States about the year 1820 or 1825. The Turners of Bay Verte are among his lineal descendants. Rev. E. C. Turner, of the New Brunswick and Prince Edward Island Conference, belongs to this family.

## ROACH.

Thomas Roach was born in 1768, in Cork, Ireland, where he spent his early years. He was educated for the priesthood, and could speak fluently in several languages. About the year 1790 he accompanied his father to Nova Scotia and settled in Fort Lawrence. The elder Mr. Roach did not remain long in Nova Scotia, but pushed on to New York. His son never heard from him after they parted at Halifax. Thomas Roach was very successful in business and for many years was one of the leading men in the Methodist Church on the Isthmus. He was elected a representative to the Provincial Parliament five times in succession, and served the people in that capacity from 1799 to 1826.

Mr. Roach was married four times. His family of four sons and three daughters was the fruit of his first marriage. Ruth, daughter of Charles Dixon, Sackville, was his first wife; his second, Mrs. Sarah Allen; third, Mary Dixon, of Onslow, and his fourth, Charlotte Wells. Mr. John Roach, of Nappan, and Dr. Roach, of Tatamagouche, are grandsons of Thomas Roach.

## SILLIKER.

William Silliker was a U.E. Loyalist from Connecticut, and came to Bedeque, P.E. Island, in 1783, where he spent the last years of his life. His son, William C. Silliker, moved to Bay Verte in the early part of the last century. This son was a master mariner, and spent most of his life at sea. He married Amelia Chappell, and had a family of three children, two sons and one daughter. The Sillikers of Bay Verte are descended from Captain Silliker. Alderman Silliker of Amherst also belongs to this family.

## HEWSON.

James Hoytte Hewson and his mother came to Nova Scotia in 1783 with a party of Loyalists, and settled in Wallace. His father, Richard Hewson, who was an officer in the British army, was killed in a negro insurrection in the south. Mrs. Hewson and her young son were sent north to live with friends, which explains how they came to be with the Loyalists. Mrs. Hewson's maiden name was Hoytte. They soon sold their property in Wallace and removed to Fort Cumberland, then one of the centres of trade in the new country. Here Mrs. Hewson opened a little store and also taught a school, and her son worked as clerk for Titus Knapp. Mrs. Hewson was successful in her trade venture, and in 1796 she and her son bought from Spiller Fillimore his farm on Jolicure Point, which has been known ever since as the Hewson farm. This property is still in possession of the family, and has been the home of four generations. James Hewson married Jerusha Freeman, of Amherst, and had six children—Richard married Seraphina Bent, of Fort Lawrence, and lived at River Philip, N.S.; James married Phebe Wry, and remained in Jolicure; William married Elizabeth Chandler, and inherited the homestead; Olive married George Darby, of Bedeque, P.E. Island; Jerusha married George Baxter, Land Surveyor, and a Loyalist, and lived in Amherst; Phebe married John Schurman, of River Philip, the grandfather of President Schurman of Cornell University, Ithaca, N.Y. John Hewson, of Jolicure, Dr. William and Watson, of Point de Bute, and Dr. Charles Hewson, of Amherst, are sons of William Hewson.

## READ.

Several persons answering to the name of Read came to the Isthmus soon after the Expulsion. Thomas Read, who was one of the Yorkshire emigrants of 1774, settled on the River Hebert. In 1786 Eliphlet Read and Joseph Read were residents of Sackville. In 1788 Stephen Read was one of the Trustees of the Stone Church

(Methodist) at Point de Bute. In 1800 an Eliphlet Read lived in Jolicure. He married a Miss Converse and had a large family. John Read, of Jolicure, and William Read,[6] of Amherst, are grandsons of this Eliphlet.

## WRY.

John Wry emigrated from Yorkshire to Nova Scotia about 1780, and settled in Sackville. He bought from William Maxwell the farm on which the Brunswick House now stands and made his home there. The Maxwells were from New England, and had been in the country some years. John Wry married a Miss Maxwell. The late Christopher Wry of Jolicure was a son of John Wry. The Wrys of Sackville are descendants of John.

## BOWSER.

Thomas Bowser was one of the Yorkshire emigration of 1774, and settled in Sackville. His son, Thomas, married Fanny King, and lived on Cole's Island. Arthur and Blair Bowser of Point de Bute and John and Bliss of Jolicure are grandsons of Thomas (second).

## LOWTHER.

Tradition says that the Lowther name was brought to England by one Colonel Lowther, in 1688. This Colonel Lowther was one of the trusted soldiers that the Prince of Orange brought with him from Holland, and was afterwards allotted an estate in Devonshire. From there the family spread to other parts of England. William Lowther, who settled in Westmoreland, N.B., came from Yorkshire, in 1817. He was accompanied by three brothers and one sister. The three brothers and the sister settled in Cumberland County, N.S. William had a family of nine children. William (second), married Lucy Chapman and settled in Great Shemogue. George married Mary Pipes and settled at the Head of Amherst. Mary married Joseph Carter, of Point de Bute. Hannah married Edward Smith, of Amherst Head. Sarah Thomasina married Rufus Carter, of Point de Bute. Rufus first married Sarah Pipes; his second wife was Elizabeth Lowther. Jane married Richard Pipes, of Nappan. Titus married Phoebe Carter, and remained in Westmoreland. Catherine married William Kever, and went to Minnesota.

## ALLAN.

Benjamin Allan was a Scotchman who came to Cumberland from the United States about the time of the Revolutionary War. There is evidence that he was with Wolfe at the taking of Quebec. If so, he was probably one of the disbanded British soldiers that found their way to Canada at the close of (sic) American War. He married a Miss Somers, of Petitcodiac, at the Bend, and finally settled at Cape

---

[6] Joseph Read, of Bay Verte, writes: William Read, from New England, came to Sackville about the year 1760. His sons were Benjamin, Joshua, Eliphalet, and William, the latter my grandfather. Grandsons: Eliphalet, William, James, Caleb, Harris, Asa, and John, the last mentioned being my father.

Tormentine.

Mrs. Allan was a very large woman, of pure Dutch stock, with, it is said, a marked tendency to stand upon her rights. Tradition also says that the pugilistic tendencies of the family were inherited from the mother, as the father was a very quiet, meek-mannered man. It might be that domestic felicity was more likely to be attained by such a demeanor. The Allan family consisted of eight sons and three daughters —Ephraim, Jonas, James, Matthew, Liff, Dan, George, and Ben were the names of the boys. It is told of Matthew that once when he was "on a time," the press gang took him and his boon companion on board a man-of-war and induced them to enlist. When the young men came to themselves they were in great trouble, and one night, when the ship was lying near one of the West India Islands, they jumped overboard with the hope of reaching the shore by swimming. Allan succeeded, and after spending some days on the island in hiding, he found a vessel which brought him back to Halifax, from which place he soon found his way home, none the worse for his experience. His companion was never heard from. A great many of the name are now living at the Cape where their ancestor first settled.

## CHAPPELL.

The Chappells were early in the country. There were two brothers, Eliphet and Jabez. Eliphet settled at Bay Verte, and had a family of four sons and five daughters. George and Bill, two of his sons, married sisters, Jane and Polly, daughters of William Wells, of Point de Bute. George's children were William, George, Joshua, Watson, Susanna, Peggy, Maria, Ann, Amelia, Almira and Jane. George married Betsy Freeze; Susanna, ——-Strange; Peggy, John Rawarth; Maria, Rufus Chappell; Amelia, Nelson Beckworth; Ann, William Fawcett; Almira, Rufus Oulten, M.D. Jane did not marry. Bill Chappell's sons were Bill, Rufus, James and Edwin. His daughters, Fanny (Mrs. Capt. Crane), Matilda (Mrs. Edward Wood), Caroline (Mrs. John Carey), Louisa (Mrs. Charles Siddall).

The Chappells were a prominent family in Bay Verte for many years, and have a good record there.

## BETTS.

Three brothers by this name emigrated from England to New York shortly before the Revolutionary War. Two of the brothers fought in that war on the English side, and in 1783 came to Nova Scotia. Isaac settled at Wallace, Cumberland, and his brother settled on the Miramichi River, in New Brunswick, where the name is still found. George Betts of Point de Bute, is a son of Benjamin and a grandson of the brother who settled at Wallace.

## IRVIN.

Joseph Irvin was another of the North of Ireland men that came to Old Cumberland early in the last century. He settled first on the north-west side of the Point de Bute ridge, where the road makes a slight angle to cross the marsh to Jolicure.

Here he and his friend, Isaac Doherty, kept a store and built a vessel. The locality was called Irvin's Corner in the early days. Mr. Irvin married Ann Tingley, and soon after moved to Tidnish, where he spent the remainder of his life as a farmer. His family consisted of seven sons and three daughters. Three of his sons, Joseph, Edwin and James, now represent the name in Tidnish.

## HAMILTON.

Robert Hamilton was born in Tyrone County, Ireland, and emigrated to New Brunswick in the year 1824, settling at Tidnish. He had a family of four children, Gustavus, Mary, Eliza and Eleanor. His son, Gustavus, married Eleanor Goodwin, and remained on the home farm, which is now owned by his son, Isaac G. Hamilton. Rev. C. W. Hamilton, of St. John, and Dr. Hamilton, of Montreal, are grandsons of Robert Hamilton. Robert Hamilton had a brother, Gustavus, who was a Methodist local preacher, and for many years was a valuable assistant to the regular minister at Point de Bute when that circuit included the present Bay Verte circuit.

## FORMER RESIDENTS OF OLD CUMBERLAND, NONE OF WHOSE DESCENDANTS OF THE NAME LIVE THERE NOW

BURNS.—John Burns was from Ireland. He came to New Brunswick in the early part of the last century, and settled at Mount Whatley. He married a Miss Harrison, and had a family of six children. He carried on a large and profitable mercantile business for a number of years. There are none of the name here at present.

PAGE.—William Page lived at Mount Whatley for some years in the early part of the last century, and carried on quite an extensive business in wood-work and dry goods.

SMITH.—Dr. Rufus Smith lived near Fort Cumberland and had a large medical practice on the Isthmus. He belonged to one of the Loyalist families, and represented the County of Westmoreland in the Assembly at Fredericton for a period of fifteen years, from 1816. His remains lie in the cemetery at Point de Bute.

CHANDLER.—Col. Joshua Chandler, of New Haven, graduated at Yale College in 1747. He was a member of the Connecticut Legislature. Being loyal, he left when Gen. Tryon, was obliged to evacuate that place. His property was valued at £30,000 sterling, and was confiscated. He settled with his family at Annapolis, N.S. He and two daughters and a son were ship-wrecked going from Digby to St. John, in March, 1787. The son was drowned in his efforts to swim to the land, while the father and the two daughters perished from cold and exposure after they had reached the shore. The British Government allowed the surviving children, Sarah, Mary, Thomas, Samuel and Charles, each £1,000 sterling. Sarah married Wm. Botsford, father of the late Judge Wm. Botsford, and grandfather of Senator Botsford; Mary married Col. Joshua Upham, afterwards Chief Justice of New Brunswick. Thomas Chandler, M.P.P., a lawyer of eminence, died at Pictou. His wife, Elizabeth Grant, was an aunt of Sam. Slick, whose name was Thomas Chandler

Haliburton. Samuel Chandler was also in the Legislature of Nova Scotia for many years, representing Colchester County. He married Susan Watson. His eldest son was the late Judge James W. Chandler, of Westmoreland, Charles H. Chandler was Sheriff of Cumberland for thirty-eight years. Among his children were Sheriff Joshua Chandler, of Amherst, and the late Lieutenant-Governor E. B. Chandler, of Dorchester. The three sons of Col. Joshua Chandler in the early part of the last century, lived in the township of Cumberland for a time and conducted a general trading business. Their brother-in-law, William Botsford, was also a resident of the township at the same time.

McMonagles.—The McMonagles lived for a time in Cumberland and afterwards moved to Sussex, where the name is still found.

Forster.—George Forster was from Yorkshire and settled in Amherst, N.S. One of his sons settled in Fort Lawrence, and another, Ralph, in Point de Bute. Ralph subsequently went to Upper Canada. The Forsters were Methodists, and it is doubtful if any of that Yorkshire band of Bible loving men and women equalled the Forsters in their veneration for the Word of God and its teachings as they understood it.

Carey.—The Careys belonged to the Scotch-Irish immigration that came to Eastern Canada between 1815 and 1830. The family landed here about the year 1822. Robert settled near Halifax; John came to New Brunswick and bought a property at Port Elgin, near the village of Bay Verte, where he built a grist and carding mill, and successfully conducted a large business for many years. He married Caroline Chappell and had a family of seven children. There are some of the descendants, but none of the name living in Bay Verte at this date. Leslie Carey, of Sackville, and Everett Carey, of California, are grandsons of John Carey.

## DOHERTY.

Rexton, Kent, July 4th, 1902.

Dear Sir,—Yours to hand yesterday, and in reply I have to state that the widow Doherty (my grandmother) left the Parish of Rag, County Donegal, Ireland, about the year 1820, and landed with her family in Magudavic, walked to St. John, N.B., and eventually got by schooner up to Great Village, N.S., except my father, William, who remained for some time longer in St. John, but also got to Great Village, N.S., and gradually worked his way to Richibucto, where he had an aunt (Mrs. John McGregor, and sister to Mrs. Joseph Irvin, of Point de Bute or Tidnish). My grandmother likely found her way for a time with part of her large family to Point de Bute, where one of her daughters (Jane) married Richard Jones, of that place. One of her daughters (Mary) remained in Nova Scotia and married George Spencer, and after a number of years moved to Mill Branch, Kent, N.B. Grisilda, the eldest daughter, married John Reid, but I do not know when married, but they resided in Mill Branch, Kent County, from my earliest recollection. My father, William, in time settled on a farm on the main Richibucto River, and married Nancy McLeland, of Great Village, N.S., a sister of G. W. McLelland, who for many years represented Colchester County in the House of Assembly at Halifax. My father afterwards moved to the south branch of the St. Nicholas River, Kent County, and built an extensive establishment of mills, including saw, grist and carding mills. Joseph Doherty, the youngest of the family, located in Buctouche, where he also established a mill property, now in possession of John McKee, but subsequently removed to Campbellton. Isaac Doherty, the eldest of the family, came to Canada some five years before his mother and the rest of the family, and he and Joseph Irvin conducted some trade with Newfoundland, and, I think, built a ship somewhere about Tidnish or Bay Verte. Isaac and Joseph married sisters, the former Cynthia, and the latter Polly Wells.

After my father, William, got settled on the main Richibucto River, his mother and youngest brother, Joseph, resided with him; so I don't think that the family, except Isaac and Jane, remained very long in Point de Bute. My grandfather's name was William, but he never came to America. My grandmother's maiden name was Marjorie Fetters. You can see that the Doherty family, with the exception of Isaac and Jane, were not actually settlers or permanent residents of Point de Bute. Both Isaac and Jane (Mrs. Jones) are buried there. Perhaps the Irvin family can add other facts to what I have written. With kind remembrance to self and family, I remain.

Yours very truly,
J. W. DOHERTY, M.D.

HOWARD TRUEMAN, ESQ.
Prospect Farm,
Point de Bute.

## LATER RESIDENTS OF WHAT WAS THE OLD TOWNSHIP OF CUMBERLAND.

McCREADY. — HIGGINS. — C. F. McCready's and David Higgin's ancestors were Loyalists. The McCreadys settled in King's County, N.B., and Higgins, in Colchester, N.S.

SNOWDON. — The Snowdons were originally from Wales, England. Pickering Snowdon was a resident of Sackville in 1786.

SUTHERLAND. — James Sutherland is of Scotch blood. Donald Sutherland, his grandfather, came from Sutherlandshire, Scotland, in 1818, and settled in Pictou County, N.S.

BULMER. — George Bulmer is a descendant of George Bulmer, who came from

Yorkshire in the ship *Duke of York* in the spring of 1772. He came with his brother-in-law, William Freeze. The Bulmers are said to be of Norman descent.

FULLERTON.—Douglas Fullerton's grandfather was a Scotchman, coming to Halifax about the year 1790. He taught school for a number of years. He married a Miss Peck and soon after settled down as a farmer in Parrsboro', Cumberland County, N.S., where many of his descendants live.

DOYLE.—James Doyle's grandfather came from Ireland and settled at Five Islands, Colchester County, N.S.

HICKS.—This name was early in Nova Scotia. I find John Hicks in company with three others, prospected Nova Scotia, in 1759, for prospective settlers, from Rhodes (sic) Island and Connecticut, and decided to take up lands at Pisquid or Windsor. Josiah Hicks was a resident of Sackville in 1786. The late Samuel Hicks of Jolicure came to that place from Sackville where the name is now in large number.

Lector House believes that a society develops through a two-fold approach of continuous learning and adaptation, which is derived from the study of classic literary works spread across the historic timeline of literature records. Therefore, we aim at reviving, repairing and redeveloping all those inaccessible or damaged but historically as well as culturally important literature across subjects so that the future generations may have an opportunity to study and learn from past works to embark upon a journey of creating a better future.

This book is a result of an effort made by Lector House towards making a contribution to the preservation and repair of original ancient works which might hold historical significance to the approach of continuous learning across subjects.

HAPPY READING & LEARNING!

LECTOR HOUSE
**LECTOR HOUSE LLP**
E-MAIL: lectorpublishing@gmail.com